SAGE STERLING
IN BUSINESS:

SAGE STERLING IN BUSINESS:

2nd Edition

David Woodford

SIGMA PRESS – Wilmslow, United Kingdom

This edition first published in 1993 by
Sigma Press, 1 South Oak Lane, Wilmslow, Cheshire SK9 6AR, England.

British Library Cataloguing in Publication Data
A CIP catalogue record for this book is available from the British Library.

ISBN: 1-85058-507-5

Typesetting and design by
Sigma Press, Wilmslow

Printed in Malta by
Interprint Ltd

Distributed by
John Wiley & Sons Ltd., Baffins Lane, Chichester, West Sussex, England.

Foreword

Mardells Limited is a company in the thick of the building industry with all that that implies in terms of 'ups and downs' of trade.

We started off as a 'one man band', but quickly developed from there and within the space of one year became a multi-million pound turnover company. As a result our bookkeeping just couldn't cope, and we had no idea where we were or even if we were making a profit or a loss! We then contacted David Woodford for help, and he quickly identified our needs – to get control of our business. He introduced us to SAGE Accounting which seemed to have the answers for us.

David spent a lot of time with us training us in the use of SAGE and showing us how it could benefit Mardells. The value of this came into its own when the recession hit the building industry in 1991. Competitors were 'falling like flies' around us, but we managed to keep our head above water because of the information forthcoming from SAGE.

Firstly, our bank had confidence in us because they could see we knew what we were doing and how we were progressing. Secondly we ourselves could make reasoned decisions (sometimes quite hard and difficult ones) because we knew exactly what our position was.

And so, we weathered the storm and survived when others didn't. We can confidently say that SAGE played a major part in that, as did the clear and succinct explanations of its working that David Woodford gave us.

The Directors; Mardells Ltd, Stevenage, Herts

Preface to the Second Edition

This Second Edition of "Sage Sterling in Business" has some additional features, as well as a few minor adjustments to some of the instructions. In particular, we have now included a much-requested chapter on the Invoicing feature in Financial Controller, explaining how to get the best from this module.

Also, Version 5 of the Sterling range has now been released with a number of significant updates of features and these have ben included in this edition of the book. For ease of reference – and to enable the reader to find what applies to his version of the program easily – this symbol:

V 5 appears in the text whenever there are changes in Version 5 which significantly alter the way in which information is accessed or recorded.

This book is already established as an easy-to-follow and comprehensive review of the Sage Sterling accounting programs, and this new edition will be even more useful to our intended audience.

David Woodford

Preface to the First Edition

"Let's computerise the accounts!", says the Managing Director one morning.

For many companies, these words have been the start of a long, painful and arduous process causing much heartache, frayed tempers, and in some cases serious financial problems.

We aim to show through the pages of this book that by careful forethought, some advance planning and correct decisions-making, such a process can bring many benefits to a company, and that nearly every difficulty can easily be avoided.

The writer is a Manager who has learnt about computers, not a computer-man who has learnt about managing. This is important, because it means that we shall be using plain English and seeing matters from the reader's point of view, and trying to avoid 'computer-ese' wherever possible.

Not only that, the writer has worked as a freelance consultant with a variety of companies who have introduced computerised accounting and seen the advantages it has brought them... and the pitfalls into which they have fallen!

All of this has been distiled into this book which we hope will help you to understand not just the SAGE software, but the reasons behind the actions you will take. This we firmly believe will give you the freedom to use SAGE with understanding – as a very useful tool to improve your profitability, and to control your business.

CONTENTS

1

Why Computerise your Accounts?

Before we go any further, let's examine WHY you (or the Managing Director, or the Accountant) might want to computerise the accounts.

Is it because:

'everyone else is doing it'? or

'we've got space on the computer'?, or

'it's about time we did it'? or

'our manual system is in a mess'?

If it's any of these – PLEASE DON'T DO IT! – (at least, not yet). It will cause you frustration and despair. Not because the software systems are difficult, but because you will not have sufficient motivation with these reasons to see you through the so-called 'learning curve' during the early stages. You will have committed yourself and your company to an unfamiliar system, which may not even be the right one for you.

And very likely you will have stopped using your old manual system in favour of this new one and will find it almost impossible to pick up the threads again.

Can you imagine the mess that will cause? Can you imagine the problems you will face? Can you imagine how that will affect your business? DON'T DO IT for those reasons! Far better you sort out the existing system with qualified help and human resources than chart the unknown waters of computerisation at this stage.

However, if the reasons are among the following, then read on:

'our manual system is taking us too long';

'I don't know whether we've made a profit or a loss until the end of the year';

'I don't know who owes us what and for how long.';

'we need to control our expenses'

These reasons are what you need to succeed. All of these (and much more besides) will come when you computerise, and you will see it through to get the results.

YOU ARE THE ONE WHO NEEDS THIS BOOK.

What computerisation of your accounts will give you will include:

accuracy of calculations;

uniformity of entry;

consistency of presentation;

meaningful reports;

financial control of your business;

facts on which to base decisions

Specifically you can extract the following information on a regular basis:

transaction histories on each of your customers;

comprehensive lists of overdue accounts and the length of time outstanding;

regular production of Statements to selected accounts;

'bespoke' letters to chase payments;

easy processing of invoices and payments;

information on which of your suppliers you owe money to, and since when;

production of Remittance Advices when paying;

a regular statement of your company's performance and assets/ liabilities;

a regular print out of actual performance against Budget;

production of a Trial Balance at any time;

a full record of Bank movements over a specified period;

the ability to automate the VAT returns every quarter;

complete control over your component stocks, and valuations of them;

a comprehensive Sales Order Processing package

..... and very much more besides.

If you feel that this is what you need to gain control of things, or you are charged with the job of obtaining this information for your manager, then you can undertake the task with confidence.

IT WILL WORK FOR YOU – you have the right motivations.

Now you are ready to consider the information which is to follow.

Which System Shall We Buy?

The choice of accounting systems for the computer is amazing! They range in price from less than £100 to many thousands of pounds.

Why? How do they differ? Do you 'get what you pay for' in software? Let's address these questions in this chapter and see if we can make an informed choice as to the most suitable for your company – because at the end of the day that is what it is about – what is best for YOU.

Accounting systems fall into three broad categories, viz:

Cash Book systems;

Integrated systems;

Modular systems

To understand the difference and know what you want we need to take a small diversion into the realms of accountancy (if you understand the difference between Sales, Purchase and Nominal Ledgers then you can skip this bit).

If we might use an illustration drawn from a familiar situation it might help.

In virtually every office using manual accounting you will find Ledgers consisting of (often) a box full of cards for each of your customers and/or suppliers. On these cards appear details of all invoices raised, the date of payment, and things like credit limits, contacts etc. This we can call the Sales and Purchase Ledgers. They usually are only used for goods bought and sold on credit.

However, you may also be familiar with a handwritten ledger book that looks something like this:

PURCHASE LEDGER for MONTH of January 1992...........

Date	Details	Gross Amount	V A T	Direct Purchases	Car Expenses	Print P & S	Gas Electricit	Rent	Misc.
1 Jan	Magnetic Supplies	293.75	43.75	250.00					
2 Jan	Esso garage	15.00	2.23		12.77				
3 Jan	Rent	350.00	52.13					297.87	
5 Jan	Eastern Electricity	298.52	-				298.52		
6 Jan	J Smith & Co	440.63	65.63	375.00					
13 Jan	The Print Shop	19.63	2.92			16.71			
15 Jan	Esso garage	15.00	2.23		12.77				
19 Jan	C Jones Ltd	17.50	2.60						14.90

Figure 2.1 Handwritten Ledger

You will note how each entry has been analysed over different headings so that the total expended on each of these categories can be calculated every month, every quarter etc.. This you might consider to be the NOMINAL LEDGER.

Now back to our discussion of the different types of accounting systems.

Types of Systems

Cash Book Systems

This, in its simplest form duplicates the operation of the Nominal Ledger system we have described above. You can have many more analysis headings than on paper systems, and the additions and subtractions etc. are obviously much more accurate.

Each system differs in the features it offers, but with many you need to understand which headings need to be credited and which debited. Additionally, this type of program in the main does not cater for credit sales or purchases.

However, if your accounts are very simple and you do very little credit sales, then this system would be very suitable.

Anything more complex would require one of the remaining two systems:

Integrated Systems

This means that all three ledgers (Sales, Purchase and Nominal) are tied in together. Whenever an entry is made into the Sales Ledger, for instance, the necessary Nominal Headings are also updated, including the Bank Account and VAT reconciliation.

This has the advantage that you need never have to recall which accounts to credit or debit etc., since the system remembers that for you.

There are, however, two things to look out for which you need to aware of:

FIRSTLY: once a ledger is closed for the month end, then ALL ledgers have to be closed i.e. you cannot then hold open the Purchase Ledger until all invoices are received as you can with a manual system.

SECONDLY: in common with many computerised systems at this level, once a Sales or Purchase Invoice has been fully paid , then after the current month end, all details of it are wiped clean. Therefore, unlike a manual ledger card you do not have an historic record. This disadvantage can be overcome somewhat by ensuring that a full print out is produced every month.

This type of accounting system is ideal for small to medium size companies who have credit sales and so on.

The third type of system is:

Modular Systems

Again, this maintains separate Sales, Purchase and Nominal Ledgers, but updating only takes place when you decide.

This has the advantage that you can hold open one ledger after others have been closed. But it has the disadvantage that you must remember to order the update of ledgers at predetermined times.

Additionally these type of systems often allow for transactions in a variety of foreign currencies.

Quite obviously this type of system gives greater flexibility, and often (but not always) is used in larger organisations.

So having considered these facts (which have been deliberately simplified) let us move to the next stage:

Which one will you choose?

There is no 'right and wrong' answer to this! Firstly you must sit down and ask: what do I want my systems to do? Who will operate it? What is their level of experience in both accounts and keyboard skills? How important is this feature or that feature? And so on.

THEN (and only then) can you make a decision.

Make a list of the functions that you want and give them a 'priority' score, say 5 for 'essential', 4 for 'would like' etc. Then look at the published specifications of the programs you are interested in and see how nearly they meet your list. From this, together with price considerations and the performance ability of your computer, you should be able to determine the system that most nearly meets your needs.

In this publication we are concentrating on the INTEGRATED SYSTEM, since we believe it offers the best combination of ease of use and economy, yet providing a very useful management tool.

And, of these systems, we are writing about the SAGE Sterling range of accountancy software.

The writer has no connections with SAGE, and has no particular bias to any one system. However, he has found SAGE to be a very easy system to use and install, and has also found the after-sales support from SAGE to be of a very high level. For these reasons we are concentrating our attention on this system, but many of the principles can be applied in other similar packages.

We propose, in this book, to write about SAGE Financial Controller, and to concentrate on the SALES & PURCHASE LEDGERS, the NOMINAL LEDGER, and the UTILITIES functions. Most of the other products in the Sterling range also offer these facilities so in most cases what is said here also applies to: Accountant and Accountant Plus.

This will give you a good working knowledge of the system, and then we hope, in a later book, to cover the extra features, such as STOCK CONTROL, SALES ORDER PROCESSING and REPORT GENERATOR.

However, we have found that whilst the SAGE manuals are technically very correct, they do not take the novice through the basics of setting up and running a 'real life' system. Therefore, what we propose to do in this publication is to explain how a fictitious company (we shall call it 'ACE Supplies') installs SAGE Financial Controller on its IBM-compatible PC and begins its day-to-day running of the system.

For the purposes of this book, 'ACE Supplies' sell computer consumables, and provide some consultancy services to their customers.

So now, let us assume that 'ACE Supplies' have made their selection of accountancy software and have decided on SAGE Financial Controller, and let us begin to explain the steps they take to get a fully working computerised accountancy system.

3

Early Steps

On opening the box supplied from SAGE you will find:

four 5.25" disks, two 3.5" disks, three manuals and various other papers.

There are two things to do straight away before anything else:

The FIRST is to take copies of the master disks in whatever format your computer uses. (The easiest way to do this is to use the DISKCOPY command in DOS — see your computer manual if you are not sure about this).

These copies will be your working copies, not the originals. Take the originals and place them somewhere safe — either in a fire-proof receptacle, or somewhere other than the premises in which the computer is located.

The SECOND thing to do is to locate the SAGE Registration Card. Fill in the Serial Number to be found on your Master Disks and send the card off — this entitles you to 90-day free support from the SAGE Helpline. (As to whether you subscribe to extending this support is up to you — but for your subscription you will continue to receive Helpline assistance, you will get free updates of the program as and when made, and free information sheets from time to time.)

Having taken these very important steps we now come to the installation process. May we suggest that you read through this section first, noting the information which is required so that you have it to hand when you actually commit yourself on your own computer?

There is nothing more frustrating than having to either keep stopping during installation, or to having to re-install because of having inputted incorrect information.

Conventions

Let us explain the conventions we shall use in describing operations throughout the book: Keyboard input, such as "SAGELOAD" should be typed in as shown (usually the use of upper or lower case is not important) but WITHOUT THE INVERTED COMMAS (" ").

Keyboard commands such as [CR] meaning Carriage Return (or Enter), [Alt] (meaning the 'Alt' key to the left of the main alphabetic keys) should be just pressed without the [ ] symbols.

When referring to Menu selections (see later) we shall separate each selection with a slash '/' – so 'Utilities/Month End/Depreciation' would indicate the various selections on each of the sub-menus appearing after each entry.

Installation

So now, taking the Disk 1 "Install", place it in Drive A – the floppy disk slot (we shall assume for the purposes of this publication that you have a computer with a hard disk or hard card, plus one floppy drive -whilst it is possible to operate otherwise this will be the easiest and most efficient way to run).

Now change to Drive A (type "A:"[CR]) Type "SAGELOAD" [CR] After a message telling you about the installation procedures, press any key to continue.

Then, the menu in Figure 3.1 appears:

```
MSDOS Version 3.20

Select which SAGE program you wish to install

A).     Bookkeeper
B).     Accountant
C).     Accountant Plus
D).     Financial Controller
E).     Payroll II
F).     Job Costing

Which option (A-F) ?
```

Figure 3.1: Installation Menu

As 'ACE' are installing Financial Controller then enter as follows: "D" [CR] (or the letter for whichever Sterling program you are installing) The next menu then appears as follows:

```
Select the type of install procedure required

A).     Create completely new working program installation
B).     Update program files only, saving existing setup and data

Which option (A-B) ?
```

Figure 3.2: Installation Menu

Option (B) will only be used when updating an existing program, so choose "A" [CR].

Now SAGE wants to know information about your computer, so another menu appears:

```
Select the type of computer system

A).   MS-DOS standalone PC
B).   MS-DOS network
C).   Concurrent DOS XM v6 or CDOS 386


Which option (A-C) ?
```

Figure 3.3: Installation Menu

Unless you have reason to know otherwise, then enter "A" [CR].

Yet another menu appears:

```
Select your computer type

A).     IBM PC or Compatible
B).     Apricot PC
C).     Apricot XI
D).     Apricot XEN
E).     RML Nimbus PC/HD
F).     Wang PC/HD

Which option (A-F) ?
```

Figure 3.4: Installation Menu

Here you must know what computer you have, although in most cases "A" [CR] is the likely selection.

This is followed by the menu in Figure 3.5:

```
Select your disk drive configuration

A).    Single floppy drive
B).    Double floppy drive
C).    Hard disk drive

Which option (A-C) ?
```

Figure 3.5: Installation Menu

For reasons stated earlier, "C" [CR] is the preferred selection, and in any event choosing "A" or "B" will cause the program to terminate if you are using an XT computer.

Now follows a message about FILES, and BUFFERS and CONFIG.SYS, which need not concern you. Then, this message appears:

```
Please select the default directory names unless you have good reason not
to
Please enter your drive letter and sub-directory, or press ENTER to
select the defaults
```

Let us pause here a moment to consider what is being recommended.

Firstly if you do not understand about Directories and their structures then you should most certainly accept the suggested defaults offered by SAGE from this point on. And even if you do understand, it is still recommended that you follow the default suggestions.

This will result in a directory structure consisting of:
\SAGE\COMPANY0\ACCDATA

where SAGE will contain the main operating files, 'COMPANY0', some sample layouts, and 'ACCDATA', the accounts data files.

If you are using Financial Controller and want to set up additional companies within it, then you will have further sub-directories \COMPANY1, \COMPANY2 etc. each with ACCDATA sub-directories.

This is by far the most efficient way of housekeeping, and unless you have very good reasons not to follow it, we strongly recommend that you do.

So just enter [CR] for each of the following selections:

```
Destination Drive [C]: [CR]
Destination Path C:[\SAGE]: [CR]
```

The following message appears:

```
Please enter the name and address of your new company
```

Note that this will be printed on statements, pay-slips and so on, so be sure to enter it correctly

```
Enter Name? "ACE SUPPLIES" [CR]
Address Line 1:"123 HIGH STREET"[CR]
Address Line 2:"ANYTOWN"[CR]
Address Line 3:"ANY COUNTY"[CR]
Address Line 4:"AB1 2CD"[CR}
```

Quite obviously at this point you must enter correctly and carefully the details requested peculiar to your own company.

After you have entered this information, SAGE proceeds with the remainder of the installation routine, requesting various disks in turn, until it comes to selecting a printer. Then this menu appears:

```
Select printer type:

A).  DIABLO       Diablo or Compatible Daisy Wheel Printer
B).  EPSON        EPSON or Compatible
C).  HPPC         HP LaserJet (PC character set)
D).  HPROMAN8     HP LaserJet (Roman-8 character set)
E).  IBM          IBM Graphics or Compatible
F).  OKI          OKI or Compatible
G).  TANDY        Tandy DMP 130


Which option (A-G) ?
```

Figure 3.6: Installation Menu

Obviously there is going to be a big variation here between our readers and the printers they have. If you are not sure what type your printer is, refer to your printer manual; usually it will state its compatibility. If not, and it is a dot matrix printer then accept EPSON ("B" [CR]), which will work in most cases. Your choice of printer can be changed at a later stage, or indeed you can add another printer now, giving you a choice when you come to a print-out.

SAGE continues again, until decisions have to be made concerning the number of Ledger Accounts that need to be opened. So let's just think about these points before we make our selections.

Undoubtedly you will have a rough idea of the number of Sales and Purchase Ledger accounts you have (i.e. how many people you sell on credit to, and the number you buy from), and therefore can estimate the total you will need for the coming year (Note: you can easily increase this number at any time during the year, so there is no need to overestimate the figure).

As to Nominal Ledger Accounts – it really depends on the extent to which you want to analyse your income and expenditure. In most cases 100 will be more than ample, but in special cases 150 should suffice.

In the case of 'ACE Supplies' we shall show the figures we are entering in the following menus – just substitute your own:

```
Enter the number of Sales Ledger Accounts: "100"[CR]
Enter the number of Purchase Ledger Accounts: "50"[CR]
Enter the number of Nominal Ledger Accounts: "100"[CR]
```

After creating the necessary files, SAGE then requests the following information which concerns both the codes you will use for your Nominal Ledger and the Layout of Accounts (i.e. Balance Sheet and Profit/Loss Account).

If this is the first time you are using SAGE and you have no good reason for doing otherwise then we would strongly suggest that you adopt the standard default layout offered and edit it later. By doing this you will have all the Control Accounts set up correctly, and a basic layout of accounts established. It would only be if you had an existing system using a numeric code for the Nominal Ledger, or your Accountant had good reason to advise otherwise that you would not accept this.

So the menu looks like Figure 3.7:

```
Select your Nominal Ledger Account Structure:

A).   Copy the standard default layout
B).   Enter your own layout at a later date

Which option (A-B) ?
```

Figure 3.7: Installation Menu

From this point on SAGE will complete the installation without any further request for information from you, and you will be returned to the C> prompt at the finish.

Other Matters

You could now go straight into the program and start running. However, there are three areas that we would recommend you give attention to before you start, since it is so easy to forget them until you are up and running and you have started some processing, and then have to stop and go back to them.

The three things we mean are:

configuring your printer (if necessary)

setting up your Passwords;

and setting up various processing parameters, such as the number of decimal points to be used, whether invoices should contain leading zeros, and so on.

So let's spend a few minutes setting these up as well shall we?

Configuring your printer

When you selected your printer in the installation process, above, SAGE configured it to the most usual settings, and in 90% of the cases this should work for you. However just occasionally you may need to make some minor adjustments if your printer or your paper is 'non-standard.'

For Versions of SAGE before 5, you must exit the program and type INSTALL at the C:\SAGE prompt (see 'Parameters' section that follows for full details) and choose: Edit Settings/Printer Controls.

For Version 5 onwards, within SAGE chose: **Utilities/Defaults/Printer Setup**

In either case you should see a screen similar to this:

```
┌─────────────────────────────────────────────────────────────────┐
│ EPSON.PRN EPSON or Compatible                                     │
│ ─────────────────────────────────────────────────────────────    │
│ Form feed                         12   0   0   0   0              │
│ English Pound Sign 1              35   0   0   0   0              │
│ English Pound Sign 2               0   0   0   0   0              │
│ Initialise  Print 1               27  82   3   0   0              │
│ Initialise  Print 2                0   0   0   0   0              │
│ Reports     Print                 15   0   0   0   0              │
│ Report Gen. Print                 15   0   0   0   0              │
│ Invoice     Print                 18   0   0   0   0              │
│ Statement   Print                 15   0   0   0   0              │
│ Remittance  Print                 18   0   0   0   0              │
│ Letter      Print                 18   0   0   0   0              │
│ Payslip     Print                 15   0   0   0   0              │
│ Cheque      Print                 18   0   0   0   0              │
│ Giro        Print                 18   0   0   0   0              │
│ P14/P60     Print                 18   0   0   0   0              │
│ Text Editor Print                 18   0   0   0   0              │
│ Reset       Print 1               27  64   0   0   0              │
│ Reset       Print 2                0   0   0   0   0              │
│ Report      Page Length           66   0   0   0   0              │
│ Statements  Page Length / Start Line  66   0   0   0   0          │
│                                                                   │
└─────────────────────────────────────────────────────────────────┘
```

Figure 3.8 Printer Configuration Menu

Refer to your printer manual and make the changes, if necessary.

The particular areas where changes might be needed are:

if you are having problems printing out the English pound (£) sign. Then you must enter the correct control characters here (see your printer manual or handbook).

if you are using a paper for printing reports not 11" (66 characters) long. Enter the correct figure where indicated.

When you have finished, either [ESC] in the normal way (Version 5), or select 'Exit' until escaping from the program.

Passwords

With 'ACE Supplies' they have the situation of having an Accounts Clerk who does the data entry, a trainee Management Accountant whose job it is to compile management reports, and both report to the Managing Director.

The Managing Director has decided that he really does not want the Accounts Clerk to have access to the various reports of the company, but on the other hand he does not want the Management Trainee to be allowed to enter information into the computer yet as he is too inexperienced. So he decides that the following access shall be granted:

> Managing Director: All functions
>
> Trainee: All reports, no postings
>
> Accounts Clerk: All postings, no reports

So passwords are assigned to each of them as follows:

> Managing Director: RED
>
> Trainee: BLUE
>
> Accounts Clerk: GREEN

Give some serious thought to the quality of your passwords since the whole idea is to prevent unauthorised access. Using the person's name is the most obvious and therefore the most useless. In the above example there is a common theme of colour, so it too leaves something to be desired. Also make sure that passwords are not declared to unauthorised personnel, otherwise the whole object is thwarted.

So now:

> place the INSTALL disk in drive A:
>
> change your current path in C:\ to SAGE (i.e. cd\SAGE)
>
> type the following (the whole range of options is given in the SAGE Installation Manual):

```
A:PASSWORD AA RED ALL
```

(Note: no space between the "A:" and the first word.)

```
A:PASSWORD AA BLUE SP PP NP UT
```

```
A:PASSWORD AA GREEN SR PR NR UT
```

```
A:PASSWORD AD LETMEIN
```

This has the effect of Adding in the Accounts section (i.e. the AA) the specified passwords and the nominated access. It also has the effect of deleting (AD) the default password of LETMEIN.

 In Version 5 the requirement is that the Password program is copied over from the floppy disk to the Hard disk, used to change and/or alter the password, and then is de-installed.

So, in drive C:, change to the main directory in which you have installed SAGE (C:\SAGE if you have used the defaults) by typing:

cd\SAGE (or whatever directory it should be)

Then change back to the floppy drive (type **a:** for instance) and then place the Master INSTALL disk in the drive. Thereafter type:

A:INSTALLS PASSWORD.EXE [CR]

This will transfer the password program to the Hard Disk ready for use.

To use it type:

PASSWORD [type][option][menus]

where :

Type is: **A** for the Accounting module

Option is:

A to ADD a password

D is to DELETE a password

V is to VIEW a password.

Password is: the required password chosen (see above)

Menus is: one of the two letter abbreviations for the menus to be accessed by the holder of that password. The options are:

SP   Sales Ledger Postings

SR   Sales Ledger Reports

PP   Purchase Ledger Postings

PR   Purchase Ledger Reports

NP   Nominal Ledger Postings

NR   Nominal Ledger Reports

MR   Management Reports

ST   STock Control

SO   Sales Order Processing

PO   Purchase Order Processing

IV   InVoice Production

UT   UTilities

ALL **ALL** menus.

Note: a space should be entered between the "password" command and the first two parameters; between these and the password parameters; and between these and the menu parameters.

After you have completed this, the program will ask if you want to delete PASSWORD.EXE from your hard disk. ALWAYS say 'yes' to this to prevent unauthorised tampering with this important utility.

The final thing to do before proceeding to data entry is to define some parameters.

Parameters

From the directory C:\SAGE type

`INSTALL [CR]`

after a message which then requires the pressing of any key to continue, you are then requested to choose options from another menu (Figure 3.9).

Choose "D"[CR] (Edit Settings). This then presents you with a new menu (Figure 3.10) from which you can choose which settings to edit.

```
SAGE SOFTWARE INSTALLATION ROUTINE

A).  Install Terminal
B).  Install Printer
C).  Install Drive Letters
D).  Edit settings

Q).  Abandon the program
X).  Exit from program

Which Option ?
```

Figure 3.9: Setting Parameters Menu

```
EDIT SETTINGS

A).  Screen Controls
B).  Standard Keyboard Codes
C).  Special Keyboard Codes
D).  Function Key Codes
E).  Printer Controls
F).  Drive Letters
G).  Terminal Settings
H).  Periscope Program Control
I).  Accounts Program Control

J).  Keyboard Test
K).  Keyboard Auto-Setup

X).  Return to Menu

Which Option ?
```

Figure 3.10: Edit Settings Menu

Choose "I"[CR] (Accounts Program Controls).

Then follow the menu in Figure 3.11:

```
    ACCOUNTS PROGRAM CONTROL

A).  VAT Cash Accounting                    0    0    0    0    0
B).  Qty D.P / Unit D.P                      2    2    0    0    0
C).  Debtors period / Creditors period     30   30    0    0    0
D).  Invoice leading zeroes                  0    0    0    0    0
E).  Statement Default Text [D=0,G=1,I=2]    0    0    0    0    0
F).  Remittance Advice Text [D=0,I=1]        0    0    0    0    0
G).  Update with Invoice/Order No.[I=0,O=1]  0    0    0    0    0



X).  Return to Menu


Which Line ?
```

Figure 3.11: Parameters Selection

This affects how certain information is presented within SAGE. We list comments on them – the actual selections can be seen from the SAGE Installation Manual.

VAT Cash Accounting: if you have permission to use this system of VAT payment, then make sure this option is selected from the beginning.

QTY D.P/Unit D.P: how do you want quantities to be shown on invoices etc..? Do you want decimal places to be shown? e.g. do you want to show '20' or '20.00'? Select the option which gives you what you require.

Debtors period/Creditors period: this is normally set at 30 days, but can be changed if it suits you better.

Invoice leading zeros: invoice number 101 can be shown as just that or as 000101. Which do you prefer? Make your selection.

Statement Default Text: Statements sent to outstanding debtors can state "Debit" or "Goods" or "Invoice". Again select which suits your business.

Remittance Advice Text: The options are either "Debit" or "Invoice". Make your choice.

When you have completed these selections, select "X" [CR], "X[CR], and "X"[CR] to come back to the C> prompt.

| V 5 | Version 5 of SAGE allows you to make these adjustments from within the program, which is much more convenient. |

Go to: **Utilities/Defaults/Company Preferences** and the following screen will appear:

```
┌─────────────────────────────────────────────────────────────────┐
│ ┌─────────────────────────────────────────────────────────────┐ │
│ │ Financial Controller    Company Preferences    31st March 1992│ │
│ └─────────────────────────────────────────────────────────────┘ │
│                                                                   │
│   Free Format Statement      :  N    Debtors period       :  30  │
│                                                                   │
│   Include Box on VAT Return  :  N    Creditors period      :  30  │
│                                                                   │
│   Print Individual Items     :  Y    Invoice leading zeroes :  Y  │
│                                                                   │
│   Your Address on Stationery :  Y    Taxkey Default (e.g. T1) : T1│
│                                                                   │
│   New Page for every Account :  N    Statement Default Text :  D  │
│                                                                   │
│   Pause Between Pages        :  N    Remittance Advice Text :  D  │
│                                                                   │
│   Comma Separated Output     :  N    Update by Invoice/Order No.: I│
│                                                                   │
│   VAT Cash Accounting        :  N    Current or Reconfigured TB : C│
│                                                                   │
│   Quantity Decimal Places    :  2    Default Bank Account   : 1200│
│                                                                   │
│   Unit Decimal Places        :  2    Display Function Bar   :  Y  │
│                                                                   │
└─────────────────────────────────────────────────────────────────┘
```

Figure 3.12 Company Preferences Screen

This will enable you to change any of the original settings to the ones you most frequently use (of course, you may override any of these at the time of selecting them from within the program, but by setting these up now it should reduce the number of times this is necessary).

Most of these preferences have been dealt with above; any additional ones we detail below:

Free Format Statement: With this version of SAGE you can in fact design your own layout for Statements instead of using the one supplied; choose 'Y' if this is what you want to do when printing Statements.

Include Box on VAT Return: In Version 5, the VAT return is now reproduced in a similar manner to the VAT form you should complete for HM Customs & Excise. If you wish the printout to have the box rules around it, then say "Yes" here (provided your printer can print out these rules of course!)

We then pass on to:

Current or Reconfigured TB: SAGE have now introduced an alternative way to use the Trial Balance for period ends – current or reconfigured. As this selection is very important, let us give some explanations here.

As entries of any sort are made, they are posted to various Nominal Accounts. For instance, the posting of a Sales Invoice involves not only a posting to the customer account but also nominal postings consisting of:

a DEBIT of the Gross amount to the DEBTORS CONTROL

a CREDIT of the Nett amount to the Sales Account (nominal)

a CREDIT of the VAT to the Tax Account. (see Figure 6.6, later in this book)

SAGE keeps a record of these transactions accumulated as they are made, and the TRIAL BALANCE is a record of these current positions, shown as DEBITS and CREDITS, which must, by definition, balance.

When producing a Profit & Loss account, SAGE refers to the current Trial Balance to produce the year-to-date figures and by subtracting last month's balances from the current balances, it also calculates the current month accounts.

However, in the course of time, the system will have many allocated transactions. For instance: invoices which have been paid in full; and accounts with old transactions on them. So there is a provision for RECONFIGURATION, which, in effect, clears all allocated transactions and produces a 'brought forward' balance for all Nominal Accounts. This keeps the system clear of all 'dead' transactions.

With Version 5 you now have the option of deciding whether your Trial Balance will be on a CURRENT basis or a RECONFIGURED basis.

What's the difference? Let us list the advantages and the consequences:

RECONFIGURED:

ADVANTAGES	*CONSEQUENCES*
Transactions for new month (or year) can be entered before closing current period	MUST reconfigure at end of every month.
	MUST produce and reconcile VAT return before reconfiguring.
	MUST print Profit & Loss after reconfiguration but before creating Month End files.
	MUST reset turnover figures at year end by Global Changes.

CURRENT:

ADVANTAGES	*CONSEQUENCES*
Do not have to reconfigure each month.	Cannot post advance figures.
Turnover figures automatically zeroed at Year End	In printing reports you need to specify the period required (instead of accepting defaults)

If you are uncertain what is best for you, it is the author's personal opinion that it is best to select the Reconfigured Trial Balance, but to run the reconfiguration routine at the end of every month. However by consideration of the above charts you can make the decision which is best for your needs.

A Final Suggestion

May we also suggest another optional move? If you were to create another directory called TRIAL and copy the program over to there you could use this directory as a 'test bed' for any operations you are not sure about.

Run SAGE here and try out the procedure you are not sure about, and see its effect. Then when you are confident, go back to the 'real' SAGE and run this procedure.

Additionally, if you were to set up a routine of copying over your data files from the 'real' SAGE to the 'trial' SAGE at the end of every day you would also have an extra back-up location in the event of problems (we are going to spend a whole chapter on backing up later in the book since it is so important)

If you decide to do this, type the following:

```
CD\ [CR]
MD TRIAL [CR]
CD SAGE [CR]
XCOPY \*.*/s \TRIAL [CR].
```

This will produce your 'test bed' program

(With Financial Controller you could alternatively set up a second company on the menu, calling this 'Trial' using the Multico disk. In this case you would not need to carry out the above).

Also, copy the following:

```
CD\
COPY CON TRIAL.BAT [CR]
CD\SAGE\COMPANY0\ACCDATA [CR]
COPY *.DTA \TRIAL\COMPANY0\ACCDATA [CR]
^Z
```

(this last line is obtained by pressing the [Ctrl] key at the same time as the Z key)

This will produce a little batch file which can be executed to automate the copying over procedure for you.

(With Financial Controller, utilising a second company that last line would become COPY *.DTA \SAGE\COMPANY1\ACCDATA [CR]).

Now, at the end of each session, after exiting from SAGE, if you type: "TRIAL" [CR] all current data will be copied over to the trial program to bring it up to date.

After a period of time when you are fully conversant with SAGE you can delete this extra program, but for now it will prove to be very useful.

First Moves in SAGE

Now at last we are ready to start delving into SAGE proper – to use the program for our Company and to see how 'ACE Supplies' do so too.

Let's first of all load the program.

At C:> type: "SAGE" [CR]

A black and white screen then appears with your company details on it. You can either wait until it disappears on its own, or, for quicker results, press [CR]. We then have a screen requesting 'Date' and 'Password'.

Date: normally it will present you as default with the system date i.e. today's date. Usually this is fine but in some instances you may want to choose another option. Let us say, for instance, that on the 10th April you are finishing off March's entries and you now want to run off all the reports. As SAGE normally prints the chosen date on these reports, it would make more sense to enter the date as, for example, "310392" (SAGE always requires dates to be entered in the format: date month year (with no spaces and a leading zero for single numbers). This way the date of 31 March would be entered on the reports which would make later reference much easier.

Passwords: we dealt with that earlier and so you must enter the applicable one (or use LETMEIN if you have not changed from the default).

With Financial Controller we are now presented with a menu screen with a choice of companies (one of which may be 'Trial' if you have adopted our earlier suggestion) By using the arrow keys at the far right of your keyboard (making sure the Numbers Lock is off!) you can select the one on which you are going to work in this session. Press [CR] to proceed further. Now we are presented with the following menu:

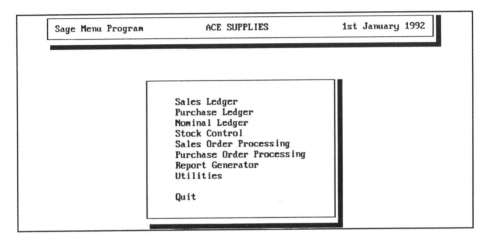

Figure 4.1: Main Menu

Menu Choice

In SAGE there are two ways to select a choice on a menu such as this: one is to use the up and down arrow keys (far right of the keyboard) until the bar marker is over the desired selection, and then press [CR]. Or to press the initial letter of the selection, which will move the cursor to the first item with that letter (be careful with Sales Ledger and Stock Control in Accountant Plus onwards as you could not get what you want with the first press of 'S').

 Version 5 now makes provision for the use of a mouse within the program (provided, of course, that the necessary drivers have been loaded beforehand to enable it to operate).

When making selections from the menus, move the cursor to the required option and click the left-hand button.

When you come to entering information in the various entry screens, pressing [CR] – the 'Enter' or the 'Carriage Return' key – will 'fix' the information in that field and move you on to the next data entry field. With the mouse, clicking the left buton will act as 'Enter' and the right as 'Escape' to move out from what you are doing at the time..

Menu Options

So let us just run over again what we mean by the various options available to us on this opening menu.

Sales Ledger: this is for all goods/services sold on credit – i.e. where payment is made some time after the transaction.

Purchase Ledger: where goods/services are bought on credit i.e. paid for some time after the transaction.

Nominal Ledger: all other transactions of the business. For instance, 'ACE Supplies' sometimes sell goods on a cash-with-order basis. There is no point in opening up a separate Sales Ledger account in this instance – it can go straight through the Bank or Cash transactions in the Nominal Ledger. Also things like Petty Cash, Director's loans, etc. properly go through the Nominal Ledger.

Report Generator: if you need special information to be extracted from SAGE which is not covered in the reports already supplied. then this powerful feature lets you create your own.

Utilities: various facilities for 'housekeeping' in SAGE, which we detail later.

You will find that each of these menus has at least one if not more sub-menus which narrow down the options which you can choose. To escape to the menu above, press the [ESC] key (top left on the keyboard).

At the end of most of these menu and sub-menus you will come to a data entry screen, which we will discuss in detail later.

Setting Up the Nominal Codes

Before we can proceed further we need to set up certain matters within SAGE so that it can be customised for our company.

So now choose: Nominal Ledger/Accounts List (i.e. Nominal Ledger, then Accounts List) and you will be given some options. For now, accept the suggestions given (by entering [CR] after each one, until you come to the option:

`Display Print or File`

There, over type "P" [CR] (for Print), check that your printer is connected and loaded with paper, and then [CR] again to print out a list. If you have chosen the SAGE default layout it should look something like Figure 4.2:

ACE SUPPLIES   Nominal Ledger - Accounts List

Ref.	Account Name	Ref.	Account Name	Ref.	Account Name
0010	FREEHOLD PROPERTY	0011	LEASEHOLD PROPERTY	0020	PLANT AND MACHINERY
0021	P/M DEPRECIATION	0030	OFFICE EQUIPMENT	0031	O/E DEPRECIATION
0040	FURNITURE AND FIXTURES	0041	F/F DEPRECIATION	0050	MOTOR VEHICLES
0051	M/V DEPRECIATION	1001	STOCK	1002	WORK IN PROGRESS
1003	FINISHED GOODS	1100	DEBTORS CONTROL ACCOUNT	1101	SUNDRY DEBTORS
1102	OTHER DEBTORS	1103	PREPAYMENTS	1200	BANK CURRENT ACCOUNT
1210	BANK DEPOSIT ACCOUNT	1220	BUILDING SOCIETY ACCOUNT	1230	PETTY CASH
2100	CREDITORS CONTROL ACCOUNT	2101	SUNDRY CREDITORS	2102	OTHER CREDITORS
2109	ACCRUALS	2200	TAX CONTROL ACCOUNT	2201	VAT LIABILITY
2210	P.A.Y.E.	2211	NATIONAL INSURANCE	2230	PENSION FUND
2300	LOANS	2310	HIRE PURCHASE	2320	CORPORATION TAX
2330	MORTGAGES	3000	ORDINANCE SHARES	3001	PREFERENCE SHARES
3100	RESERVES	3101	UNDISTRIBUTED RESERVES	3200	PROFIT AND LOSS ACCOUNT
4000	SALES TYPE A	4001	SALES TYPE B	4002	SALES TYPE C
4009	DISCOUNTS ALLOWED	4100	SALES TYPE D	4101	SALES TYPE E
4200	SALES OF ASSETS	4900	MISCELLANEOUS INCOME	4901	ROYALTIES RECEIVED
4902	COMMISSIONS RECEIVED	4903	INSURANCE CLAIMS	4904	RENT INCOME
4905	DISTRIBUTION AND CARRIAGE	5000	MATERIALS PURCHASES	5001	MATERIALS IMPORTED
5002	MISCELLANEOUS PURCHASES	5003	PACKAGING	5009	DISCOUNTS TAKEN
5100	CARRIAGE	5101	DUTY	5102	TRANSPORT INSURANCE
5200	OPENING STOCK	5201	CLOSING STOCK	6000	PRODUCTIVE LABOUR
6001	COST OF SALES LABOUR	6002	SUB-CONTRACTORS	6100	SALES COMMISSIONS
6200	SALES PROMOTIONS	6201	ADVERTISING	6202	GIFTS AND SAMPLES
6203	P.R. (LIT. & BROCHURES)	6900	MISCELLANEOUS EXPENSES	7001	DIRECTORS SALARIES
7002	DIRECTORS REMUNERATION	7003	STAFF SALARIES	7004	WAGES - REGULAR
7005	WAGES - CASUAL	7006	EMPLOYERS N.I.	7007	EMPLOYERS PENSIONS
7008	RECRUITMENT EXPENSES	7100	RENT	7102	WATER RATES
7103	GENERAL RATES	7104	PREMISES INSURANCE	7200	ELECTRICITY
7201	GAS	7202	OIL	7203	OTHER HEATING COSTS
7300	FUEL AND OIL	7301	REPAIRS AND SERVICING	7302	LICENCES
7303	VEHICLE INSURANCE	7304	MISC. MOTOR EXPENSES	7400	TRAVELLING
7401	CAR HIRE	7402	HOTELS	7403	U.K. ENTERTAINMENT
7404	OVERSEAS ENTERTAINMENT	7405	OVERSEAS TRAVELLING	7406	SUBSISTENCE
7500	PRINTING	7501	POSTAGE AND CARRIAGE	7502	TELEPHONE
7503	TELEX/TELEGRAM/FACSIMILE	7504	OFFICE STATIONERY	7505	BOOKS ETC.
7600	LEGAL FEES	7601	AUDIT & ACCOUNTANCY FEES	7602	CONSULTANCY FEES
7603	PROFESSIONAL FEES	7700	EQUIPMENT HIRE	7701	OFFICE MACHINE MAINT.
7800	REPAIRS AND RENEWALS	7801	CLEANING	7802	LAUNDRY
7803	PREMISES EXPENSES (MICS)	7900	BANK INTEREST PAID	7901	BANK CHARGES
7902	CURRENCY CHARGES	7903	LOAN INTEREST PAID	7904	H.P. INTEREST
7905	CREDIT CHARGES	8000	DEPRECIATION	8001	PLANT & MACHINERY DEPR.
8002	FURNITURE/FIX/FITTINGS DP	8003	VEHICLE DEPRECIATION	8004	OFFICE EQUIPMENT DEPR.
8100	BAD DEBT WRITE OFF	8102	BAD DEBT PROVISION	8200	DONATIONS
8201	SUBSCRIPTIONS	8202	CLOTHING COSTS	8203	TRAINING COSTS
8204	INSURANCE	8205	REFRESHMENTS	9998	SUSPENSE ACCOUNT
9999	MISPOSTINGS ACCOUNT				

Figure 4.2: Nominal Accounts – Default Layout

Observations

The numbers 0001 to 3999 have been allocated to the Balance Sheet, and 4000 to 9999 to the Profit/Loss Account.

Very likely there will be some things on there that you will not need, and others not there that you will need.

May we suggest that you give some thought to this and the numbering sequence you will use (see below) and then write on this sheet what changes are to be made.

Now let us make these changes.

Whilst still in Nominal Ledger, choose the option **Nominal Account Structure/Account Names**, and you will see a screen like Figure 4.3:

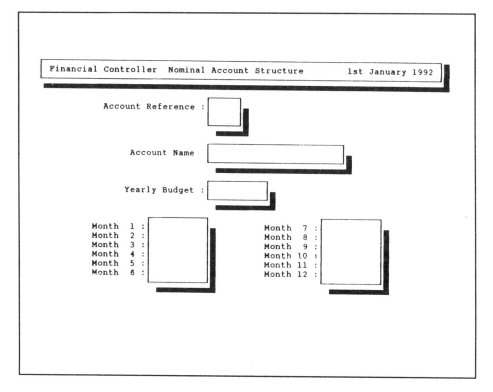

Figure 4.3: Nominal Account Names Entry Screen

For those you wish to change, type in the numeric code in 'Account Reference' and the screen in Figure 4.4 will appear:

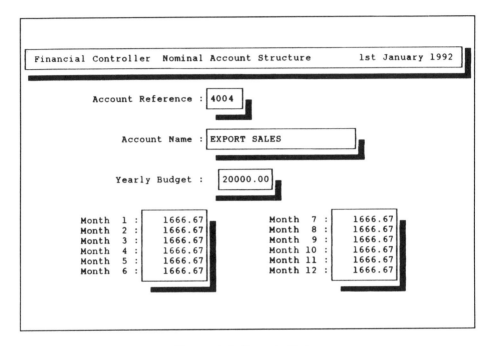

Figure 4.4: Sample Entry

In the 'Account Name' section, first press the [F8] key (i.e. function key [F8] which is either at the left or the top of your keyboard depending on which type you have) This is a short cut to delete the whole of the field rather than each character individually. Now type in the description you want.

For those new ones you wish to add , again type in the numeric code, but this time a question pops up:

`Is this a new account?`

If it is, then choose 'Yes' and make entries as above.

For those items you wish to delete entirely (and for space and convenience it is a good idea to do this), call up the same screen and number, but then hit [ESC] and select the option **DELETE** when offered, and then confirm when requested.

At the same time as making these entries you may choose to also set budgets for each one so that you may compare actual expenditure with budgeted (which is a good management policy if you want to control your business).

So move down to the 'Yearly Budget' and enter a figure here. The system will now, automatically, divide that equally over a 12 month period and insert figures for each month.

Of course, in 'real' life it doesn't work like that! Budgets tend to vary from month to month according to a whole variety of factors. No problem! Just over type in each month the figure you want for that month, and SAGE will adjust the yearly figure accordingly, until you reach the end, when it should be exactly the same total as your yearly budget for that item.

We can now show you how 'ACE Supplies' have made changes. Their Account List looks like Figure 4.5 (overleaf).

Comments

Let us make some comments about that:

1. They have bought their two vehicles on Hire Purchase some while ago, and so they wish to show the situation both on the value of the vehicle and the remaining HP obligations. So for each vehicle they have set up Nominal Codes for: the current 'written down' value of the vehicle, the depreciation, the HP Account, and (for the company auditors) the HP Interest Account (the reasons for this will become clear later when we discuss how to deal with HP transactions).

2. Also, they wish to break down their sales into: Hardware Sales (4000), Software Sales (4001), Consumables Sales (4002), Consultancy Charges (4003), and the occasional Export Sales (4004). This therefore means that the codes 4100 and 4101 are no longer needed and can be deleted.

3. For uniformity, it makes sense to use the same terminal numbers (i.e. the last two digits) for the purchases as well, as they are wanted to be shown separately. So we will use: 5000 for Hardware Purchases; 5001 for Software Purchases; 5002 for Consumable Purchases (it would not be possible to show 'purchases' for consultancy work, which is purely time related, or export sales)

4. Additionally, Code No 6002 would not be used in the business so can also be deleted.

ACE SUPPLIES   Nominal Ledger - Accounts List

Ref.	Account Name	Ref.	Account Name	Ref.	Account Name
0010	FREEHOLD PROPERTY	0011	LEASEHOLD PROPERTY	0020	PLANT AND MACHINERY
0021	P/M DEPRECIATION	0030	OFFICE EQUIPMENT	0031	O/E DEPRECIATION
0040	FURNITURE AND FIXTURES	0041	F/F DEPRECIATION	0050	FORD ACCOUNT
0051	FORD HP ACCOUNT	0052	FORD HP INTEREST ACCOUNT	0060	MERCEDES ACCOUNT
0061	MERCEDES HP ACCOUNT	0062	MERCEDES HP INTEREST A/C	1001	STOCK
1100	DEBTORS CONTROL ACCOUNT	1101	SUNDRY DEBTORS	1102	OTHER DEBTORS
1103	PREPAYMENTS	1200	BANK CURRENT ACCOUNT	1210	BANK DEPOSIT ACCOUNT
1220	BUILDING SOCIETY ACCOUNT	1230	PETTY CASH	2100	CREDITORS CONTROL ACCOUNT
2101	SUNDRY CREDITORS	2102	OTHER CREDITORS	2109	ACCRUALS
2200	TAX CONTROL ACCOUNT	2201	VAT LIABILITY	2210	P.A.Y.E.
2211	NATIONAL INSURANCE	2230	PENSION FUND	2300	LOANS
2320	CORPORATION TAX	2330	MORTGAGES	2399	DIRECTORS' LOAN ACCOUNT
3000	ORDINANCE SHARES	3001	PREFERENCE SHARES	3100	RESERVES
3101	UNDISTRIBUTED RESERVES	3200	PROFIT AND LOSS ACCOUNT	4000	HARDWARE SALES UK
4001	SOFTWARE SALES UK	4002	CONSUMABLES SALES UK	4003	CONSULTANCY INCOME
4004	EXPORT SALES	4009	DISCOUNTS ALLOWED	4200	SALES OF ASSETS
4900	MISCELLANEOUS INCOME	4901	ROYALTIES RECEIVED	4902	COMMISSIONS RECEIVED
4903	INSURANCE CLAIMS	4904	RENT INCOME	4905	DISTRIBUTION AND CARRIAGE
5000	HARDWARE PURCHASES	5001	SOFTWARE PURCHASES	5002	CONSUMABLES PURCHASES
5003	PACKAGING	5009	DISCOUNTS TAKEN	5100	CARRIAGE
5101	DUTY	5102	TRANSPORT INSURANCE	5200	OPENING STOCK
5201	CLOSING STOCK	6000	PRODUCTIVE LABOUR	6001	COST OF SALES LABOUR
6100	SALES COMMISSIONS	6200	SALES PROMOTIONS	6201	ADVERTISING
6202	GIFTS AND SAMPLES	6203	P.R. (LIT. & BROCHURES)	6900	MISCELLANEOUS EXPENSES
7001	DIRECTORS SALARIES	7002	DIRECTORS REMUNERATION	7003	STAFF SALARIES
7004	WAGES - REGULAR	7005	WAGES - CASUAL	7006	EMPLOYERS N.I.
7007	EMPLOYERS PENSIONS	7008	RECRUITMENT EXPENSES	7100	RENT
7102	WATER RATES	7103	GENERAL RATES	7104	PREMISES INSURANCE
7200	ELECTRICITY	7201	GAS	7202	OIL
7203	OTHER HEATING COSTS	7300	FUEL AND OIL	7301	REPAIRS AND SERVICING
7302	LICENCES	7303	VEHICLE INSURANCE	7304	MISC. MOTOR EXPENSES
7400	TRAVELLING	7401	CAR HIRE	7402	HOTELS
7403	U.K. ENTERTAINMENT	7404	OVERSEAS ENTERTAINMENT	7405	OVERSEAS TRAVELLING
7406	SUBSISTENCE	7500	PRINTING	7501	POSTAGE AND CARRIAGE
7502	TELEPHONE	7503	TELEX/TELEGRAM/FACSIMILE	7504	OFFICE STATIONERY
7505	BOOKS ETC.	7600	LEGAL FEES	7601	AUDIT & ACCOUNTANCY FEES
7602	CONSULTANCY FEES	7603	PROFESSIONAL FEES	7700	EQUIPMENT HIRE
7701	OFFICE MACHINE MAINT.	7800	REPAIRS AND RENEWALS	7801	CLEANING
7802	LAUNDRY	7803	PREMISES EXPENSES (MICS)	7900	BANK INTEREST PAID
7901	BANK CHARGES	7902	CURRENCY CHARGES	7903	LOAN INTEREST PAID
7904	H.P. INTEREST	7905	CREDIT CHARGES	8000	DEPRECIATION
8001	PLANT & MACHINERY DEPR.	8002	FURNITURE/FIX/FITTINGS DP	8003	VEHICLE DEPRECIATION
8004	OFFICE EQUIPMENT DEPR.	8100	BAD DEBT WRITE OFF	8102	BAD DEBT PROVISION
8200	DONATIONS	8201	SUBSCRIPTIONS	8202	CLOTHING COSTS
8203	TRAINING COSTS	8204	INSURANCE	8205	REFRESHMENTS
9998	SUSPENSE ACCOUNT	9999	MISPOSTINGS ACCOUNT		

Figure 4.5: 'Ace Supplies' Amended Nominal Accounts

Layout of Accounts

Now we have to consider the effect of these changes on the layout of accounts. If you choose: **Nominal Ledger/Nominal Account Structure/ Balance Sheet Format or Profit & Loss Format** you will see various sub-headings which you can select. Doing so reveals various Category Headings and the Nominal Codes which have been put together to form them.

In the default format, one of the layouts is as shown in Figure 4.6:

```
Financial Controller      Overheads (1)              1st January 1992


              Category Heading        Low      High
          SALARIES AND WAGES          7000     7099
          RENT AND RATES              7100     7199
          HEAT, LIGHT AND POWER       7200     7299
          MOTOR EXPENSES              7300     7399
          TRAVELLING AND ENTERTAINMENT 7400    7499
          PRINTING AND STATIONERY     7500     7599
          PROFESSIONAL FEES           7600     7699
          EQUIPMENT HIRE AND RENTAL   7700     7799
          MAINTENANCE                 7800     7899
          BANK CHARGES AND INTEREST   7900     7999
          DEPRECIATION                8000     8099
          BAD DEBTS                   8100     8199
          GENERAL EXPENSES            8200     8299
          UNUSED CATEGORY
          UNUSED CATEGORY
```

Figure 4.6: Profit/Loss Default Layout

You will note that the system is to combine, where possible, several nominal categories under one major heading. So for this, the highest and lowest codes for each heading have to be listed. Be very careful here that you do not duplicate code numbers – it is very easy to do! (If you do not understand about Balance Sheets or the layout of Profit/Loss accounts, refer this part to your Accountant.)

Adjust each of the tables (Balance Sheet: Fixed Assets/Current Assets/ Liabilities/Financed By/ Profit & Loss: Sales/Purchases/Direct Expenses/ Overheads) to take account of the changes.

In the case of 'ACE' it results in the following (Figures 4.7 and 4.8; please also compare with Figure 4.5 to see the changes made).

```
┌─────────────────────────────────────────────────────────────────────┐
│ ┌─────────────────────────────────────────────────────────────────┐ │
│ │ Financial Controller        Fixed Assets          1st January 1992│ │
│ └─────────────────────────────────────────────────────────────────┘ │
│                                                                       │
│                    Category Heading          Low       High          │
│              ┌──────────────────────────────────────────────┐       │
│              │ PROPERTY                      0010      0019  │       │
│              │ PLANT AND MACHINERY           0020      0029  │       │
│              │ OFFICE EQUIPMENT              0030      0039  │       │
│              │ FURNITURE AND FIXTURES        0040      0049  │       │
│              │ MOTOR VEHICLES                0050      0060  │       │
│              │ UNUSED CATEGORY                              │       │
│              │ UNUSED CATEGORY                              │       │
│              │ UNUSED CATEGORY                              │       │
│              │ UNUSED CATEGORY                              │       │
│              │ UNUSED CATEGORY                              │       │
│              │ UNUSED CATEGORY                              │       │
│              │ UNUSED CATEGORY                              │       │
│              │ UNUSED CATEGORY                              │       │
│              │ UNUSED CATEGORY                              │       │
│              └──────────────────────────────────────────────┘       │
└─────────────────────────────────────────────────────────────────────┘
```

Figure 4.7: Fixed Assets Layout

```
┌─────────────────────────────────────────────────────────────────────┐
│ ┌─────────────────────────────────────────────────────────────────┐ │
│ │ Financial Controller       Current Assets         1st January 1992│ │
│ └─────────────────────────────────────────────────────────────────┘ │
│                                                                       │
│                    Category Heading          Low       High          │
│              ┌──────────────────────────────────────────────┐       │
│              │ STOCK                         1000      1099  │       │
│              │ DEBTORS                       1100      1199  │       │
│              │ DEPOSITS AND CASH             1210      1299  │       │
│              │ UNUSED CATEGORY                              │       │
│              │ UNUSED CATEGORY                              │       │
│              │ UNUSED CATEGORY                              │       │
│              │ UNUSED CATEGORY                              │       │
│              │ UNUSED CATEGORY                              │       │
│              │ UNUSED CATEGORY                              │       │
│              │ UNUSED CATEGORY                              │       │
│              │ BANK ACCOUNT                  1200      1209  │       │
│              │ VAT LIABILITY                 2200      2209  │       │
│              │ UNUSED CATEGORY                              │       │
│              │ UNUSED CATEGORY                              │       │
│              │ UNUSED CATEGORY                              │       │
│              └──────────────────────────────────────────────┘       │
└─────────────────────────────────────────────────────────────────────┘
```

Figure 4.8: Current assets Layout

```
┌─────────────────────────────────────────────────────────────────┐
│ ┌──────────────────────────────────────────────────────────────┐ │
│ │ Financial Controller        Liabilities        1st January 1992│ │
│ └──────────────────────────────────────────────────────────────┘ │
│                                                                   │
│                    Category Heading          Low       High       │
│         ┌──────────────────────────────────────────────┐          │
│         │ CREDITORS : SHORT TERM           2100      2199│          │
│         │ TAXATION                         2210      2299│          │
│         │ CREDITORS : LONG TERM            2300      2398│          │
│         │ HP VEHICLES                      0070      0099│          │
│         │ DIRECTORS' LOAN ACCOUNT          2399      2399│          │
│         │ UNUSED CATEGORY                                │          │
│         │ UNUSED CATEGORY                                │          │
│         │ UNUSED CATEGORY                                │          │
│         │ UNUSED CATEGORY                                │          │
│         │ UNUSED CATEGORY                                │          │
│         │ BANK ACCOUNT                     1200      1209│          │
│         │ VAT LIABILITY                    2200      2209│          │
│         │ UNUSED CATEGORY                                │          │
│         │ UNUSED CATEGORY                                │          │
│         │ UNUSED CATEGORY                                │          │
│         └──────────────────────────────────────────────┘          │
└─────────────────────────────────────────────────────────────────┘
```

Figure 4.9: Liabilities Layout

```
┌─────────────────────────────────────────────────────────────────┐
│ ┌──────────────────────────────────────────────────────────────┐ │
│ │ Financial Controller        Financed By        1st January 1992│ │
│ └──────────────────────────────────────────────────────────────┘ │
│                                                                   │
│                    Category Heading          Low       High       │
│         ┌──────────────────────────────────────────────┐          │
│         │ SHARE CAPITAL                    3000      3099│          │
│         │ RESERVES                         3100      3299│          │
│         │ UNUSED CATEGORY                                │          │
│         │ UNUSED CATEGORY                                │          │
│         │ UNUSED CATEGORY                                │          │
│         │ UNUSED CATEGORY                                │          │
│         │ UNUSED CATEGORY                                │          │
│         │ UNUSED CATEGORY                                │          │
│         │ UNUSED CATEGORY                                │          │
│         │ UNUSED CATEGORY                                │          │
│         │ UNUSED CATEGORY                                │          │
│         │ UNUSED CATEGORY                                │          │
│         │ UNUSED CATEGORY                                │          │
│         │ UNUSED CATEGORY                                │          │
│         └──────────────────────────────────────────────┘          │
└─────────────────────────────────────────────────────────────────┘
```

Figure 4.10: Financed By Layout

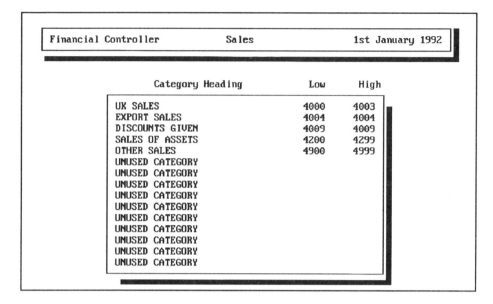

```
 Financial Controller            Sales              1st January 1992

                  Category Heading        Low     High

                  UK SALES                4000    4003
                  EXPORT SALES            4004    4004
                  DISCOUNTS GIVEN         4009    4009
                  SALES OF ASSETS         4200    4299
                  OTHER SALES             4900    4999
                  UNUSED CATEGORY
                  UNUSED CATEGORY
                  UNUSED CATEGORY
                  UNUSED CATEGORY
                  UNUSED CATEGORY
                  UNUSED CATEGORY
                  UNUSED CATEGORY
                  UNUSED CATEGORY
                  UNUSED CATEGORY
```

Figure 4.11: Sales Layout

```
 Financial Controller          Purchases           1st January 1992

                  Category Heading        Low     High

                  PURCHASES               5000    5099
                  PURCHASE CHARGES        5100    5199
                  STOCK                   5200    5299
                  UNUSED CATEGORY
                  UNUSED CATEGORY
                  UNUSED CATEGORY
                  UNUSED CATEGORY
                  UNUSED CATEGORY
                  UNUSED CATEGORY
                  UNUSED CATEGORY
                  UNUSED CATEGORY
                  UNUSED CATEGORY
                  UNUSED CATEGORY
                  UNUSED CATEGORY
```

Figure 4.12: Purchases Layout

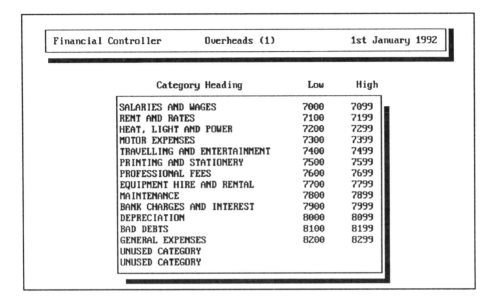

```
Financial Controller        Overheads (1)              1st January 1992


                    Category Heading         Low      High

              SALARIES AND WAGES            7000     7099
              RENT AND RATES                7100     7199
              HEAT, LIGHT AND POWER         7200     7299
              MOTOR EXPENSES                7300     7399
              TRAVELLING AND ENTERTAINMENT  7400     7499
              PRINTING AND STATIONERY       7500     7599
              PROFESSIONAL FEES             7600     7699
              EQUIPMENT HIRE AND RENTAL     7700     7799
              MAINTENANCE                   7800     7899
              BANK CHARGES AND INTEREST     7900     7999
              DEPRECIATION                  8000     8099
              BAD DEBTS                     8100     8199
              GENERAL EXPENSES              8200     8299
              UNUSED CATEGORY
              UNUSED CATEGORY
```

Figure 4.13: Overheads Layout

Note: in cases where an item can be either an Asset or a Liability (e.g the Bank Account) it should appear under both categories on the same line in both charts and in one of the last five places – SAGE will then decide where to place it in the printout.

In the event that your Balance Sheet does not balance when printing out later, you will need to print out the Trial balance (see relevant section) and then check that every item on there appears in the layout of accounts, and that nothing appears under two headings.

Changes in Version 5

 There are a number of changes in Version 5 which affect the above information. These are:

1. *Print or Display:* when preparing a report of any sort, you are now presented with a screen which shows, as standard, the defaults you have selected in Company Preferences. To alter them (for example, to Print a report where the default is to Display), enter 'C' (for **C**hange) and then move the cursor to the relevant box and over type the required initial letter (say, **D, P, F, E** – for Display, Print, File, Edit respectively).

2. *Nominal Codes entry:* New Nominal Codes can now be entered 'on the fly'. That means to say that if you need to set up a new code (or have forgotten to set one up initially) whilst entering data, you can do so without having to close down what you are doing (as previously) and go into the routine for setting up new accounts. Now you will be asked if this is a new code, and if you answer 'yes', you will drop right into the correct screen to do so then and there. After posting, you will be dropped back to the place where you left off and can continue to make entries. *However, it is important to remember that as soon as you can you should alter the Layout of Accounts (Balance Sheet or Profit & Loss Account) to take note of this addition.*

3. There is an additional feature under the Nominal Account Structure menu, called "Chart of Accounts Layout." By using this you can (a) produce a print out showing how the Balance Sheet and Profit & Loss Account will appear in use, and (b) also produce a list of Nominal Codes which have either been duplicated or missed entirely in the layout. (Choose 'Nominal Code Analysis' on the options screen to do this). This facility is extremely useful, and should be run as soon as you have completed your own layout of accounts to check it for accuracy.

Anything else we should do? Yes!

Departmental Codes

There is a facility in SAGE to use the Department Codes. These could be used to attribute costs within a company by department for instance (don't mix this up with the 'Analysis Code' in the Sales and Purchase Ledgers, which is a different analysis altogether).

Ensure that these are set up correctly, if you are going to use them, by selecting: **Utilities/Departments.**

Then choose "Edit" and make entries as required – the first one hundred numbers can be given a name, which could prove useful

Other matters

If you are using your own choice for Nominal Codes rather than the default layout, then it will also be necessary for you to set up the Control Accounts codes through the **Utilities/ Data File Utilities/ Control Accounts** option. You will need codes for: Bank Accounts, Cash Account, Debtors Control, Creditors Control, Tax Control, Mispostings Control, Retained Profit & Loss, Bad Debt Write Off , and so on.

5

Opening Balances

The first thing we must do before we can get meaningful information from the system is to enter our opening balances. Unless you are fortunate enough to be able to begin using SAGE at the start of a new financial year this step is essential. However, the degree of work involved is directly proportional to the amount of information you want to obtain from the system

The ideal situation is that you enter:

all outstanding Sales and Purchase invoices

the previous month's Trial Balance

and that is what we shall be describing

However, it may be that you do not have the Trial Balance figures (although how you could run a proper accounting system without is a mystery – you are surely computerising just in time!). In this case you may proceed without; but please note: your cumulative year-to-date figures printed out each month will be meaningless and will only be relevant to the time from which you started. They will only have value once you have completed your first year-end procedures and started anew.

What we shall be doing in entering the opening balances is as follows:

1. Entering each outstanding invoice in the Sales and Purchase Ledgers.
2. Then bringing all Nominal accounts to zero.

3. Then entering all correct Nominal account balances from the Trial Balance.

Note: *In this instance, and this instance only, we shall be making postings to the Suspense Nominal Account (No: 9998).*

So now let us proceed with the three steps.

Sales & Purchase Ledger Opening balances

Collect together all unpaid invoices as at the end of the previous month. For ease of use and double checking, bundle each set into lots of 12. With an adding machine, batch total each lot and staple the machine print-out to the batch (this is a procedure which you should really follow in all data entries).

Now call up *Sales Ledger/Customer Details.* You will there be presented with the following screen:

Figure 5.1: Customer Details Screen

This screen enables you to enter details of each of your Sales Accounts, and should be used in the future every time you open a new account.

The basic procedure is that you give each account a unique reference, and then enter the full details.

Before proceeding further let us just make a small diversion to discuss the matter of Account References.

Account References

Please give some detailed advance thought to this matter, since once you have chosen and used a system it will be very difficult to change to another.

The "Account Reference" allows you to give a 6 character alphabetic or numeric reference.

If you remember this fact: each time you want to enter Account details you must enter this Reference.

Therefore it should be easy to remember and not easily confused with others. As SAGE will do any sorting on this reference (alphabetically first), we strongly recommend that you use a mainly alphabetic system.

Here are a few suggestions:

Let us assume a company called MAGNETIC SUPPLIES.

Whilst it is possible to have a few other customers with the word 'Magnetic' in their title, there will probably not be many. So a reference such as MAGSUP will uniquely identify this customer or supplier.

However, with a customer like JOHN SMITH & CO it is quite possible that you will have a few Smiths. So more care is needed here. Two suggestions are: JSMITH or SMITH1, the latter allowing you to build SMITH2, SMITH3 etc. (SAGE can come to your help in finding the exact one as we shall explain a little later).

So we would suggest that you now sit down with a current list of customers and suppliers and give them all a unique reference.

Entering Account Details

If we now return to our screen (Figure 5.1) we can begin the entries of customer/supplier details. The information you require is as follows:

> *Account Reference:* This is the reference we have explained above, and amounts to six characters in length.

> Having entered this, SAGE will then ask:

`Is this a new account: No Yes`

> As this will definitely be new, select 'Yes'.

> *Account Name:* This gives you 25 characters in which to enter the customer/ supplier's company name.

> *Address:* Here you may use four lines each of 25 characters to enter the address details.

> *Credit Limit:* In many businesses this is used. You may set credit limits for your customers and your suppliers may do so for you. If you enter a figure here, then when printing "Account History", "Aged Debtors/ Creditors" and "Statements" a warning message will be printed if this figure has been exceeded.

> *Turnover:* This is a cumulative figure which SAGE will update for you every time an invoice is entered into the system. However, if you are just starting SAGE and you want to know this figure, then you may enter the starting total now.

> *Telephone No:* Any number up to 15 characters long.

> Contact Name: As this will be printed out on your Aged Debtors list, it could be very useful to enter it here.

> *Discount Code:* This is only of value if you are using the SAGE Invoicing procedure in conjunction with Stock Control. If so, enter either A,B, or C or D followed by a specific percentage amount e.g. D10 etc.

> *Analysis Code:* This is not an obligatory entry, but can be used as an additional analysis feature for such things as area codes, salesman's codes, product group, and so on. It allows 16 alpha numeric characters.

Once this has been accomplished, press the [ESC] key, and you will be asked:

`Do you want to: Post Edit Abandon`

If you are happy with the entry, accept 'Post'; if you want to make changes, accept 'Edit'; and if you want to start again, accept 'Abandon'.

So a typical entry for 'Ace Supplies' will look like this:

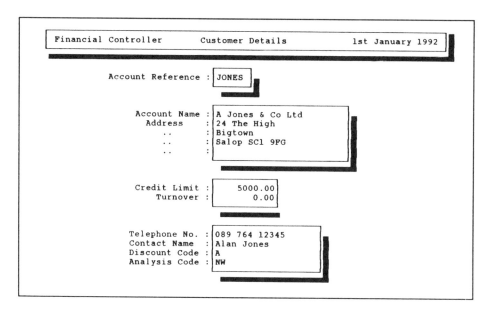

Figure 5.2: Customer Details Entry

You are then presented with the screen again, which you should use for additional entries. To return to the Main menu thereafter, press [ESC}.

Address List

It will now be useful to print out a list of this information, firstly to check the accuracy of entry, and secondly to use as a reference.

So choose "Address List", and accept the defaults offered, but overtyping "A" when asked whether you want names only or names and addresses.

Assuming everything is in order, and all accounts have now been entered, we can proceed to the actual entering of the opening balances.

Entering Opening Balances

Select **Sales Ledger/Batched Data Entry/Sales Invoices** and you will be presented with a data entry screen.

In entering opening balances use the following information:

A/c: The Account reference previously chosen (press [F4] for a full listing)

Date: Enter either the invoice date or the date on which you are entering the balance

Inv: You should enter the invoice number

N/C: For the opening balances only, you should enter the Nominal Code for the Suspense Account (using the default layout this is '9998')

Dep: No entry here

Details: This will be 'Opening balance'

Nett Amnt: This should be the nett amount on the invoice (excluding VAT)

Tc: Enter the appropriate Tax Code e.g. T1, T9 etc

Tax Amnt: The tax amount shown on the invoice.

Tips:

> The key [F6] will repeat the line directly above the one you are in;
>
> the Shift plus [F6] key will add 1 to the numeric field above the one you are in; (Version 4.2 onwards)
>
> the [F5] key will enter the system date in the date column;
>
> the [F9] key will enter the T1 tax code for you.

When the screen is full, check that the Batch Total at the top right hand corner is the same as that on your adding machine tally roll, and if it is, hit [ESC] and accept the option to POST. Continue on in this way until everything has been entered.

The effect of the above will have been to enter the correct balances on the Sales & Purchase Ledgers, and on the Creditors and Debtors Controls.

The next step now is to go back to **Nominal Ledger/Journal Entries** and post the correct Trial Balance figures which you prepared beforehand. By definition these must balance exactly to enable you to POST them and escape from the routine.

Zeroing Accounts

Since the figures which we have now entered are only for accounts outstanding, this will not give us the correct figures for the year thus far, and also will result in possible duplications. So we should now return all Nominal Accounts to zero.

To do this, first of all print out the Trial Balance.

Then go into Journal Entries (see Chapter 9) and post equal and opposite entries for each of the shown Nominal Accounts (i.e. if the Trial Balance shows a Credit, then post an equal Debit).

Attempt to produce a further print out of the Trial Balance. If you cannot (because everything is zero) then you have been successful. If you can, then you need to zero all the remaining accounts before proceeding further.

Entering Correct Trial Balance

You should have on hand the correct Trial Balance as at the end of the preceding month, either from your old system or from your accountant. By using the Journal entries procedure you should now enter these into the system (by definition, these should balance correctly to enable you to do this).

Preparing for new entries

The final step left is to get everything ready for new entries, and for ease of use we now recommend that you

a) produce a back-up disk, and

b) do a reconfiguration.

Again these procedures are dealt with in depth later, but for now, action the following:

Back-up

Place a formatted disk in drive A: of your computer.

Proceed to **Utilities/Back-up Utilities/Back-up Data Files** and accept the defaults offered. You should then after a few minutes, have obtained your back up which should now be placed in a secure location.

Reconfiguration

Go to **Utilities/Data File Utilities/Data File Changes/Reconfiguration.** Accept the defaults offered and wait until the procedure has finished.

(If you are following our earlier recommendation to have a separate 'Trial Company', now is the time also to copy over the information to this directory.

Now we are ready, at last, to begin using SAGE with real live data!

The Sales & Purchase Ledgers

In what follows, we shall deal with the Sales Ledger.

However, the procedures for the Purchase Ledger are virtually identical, and the same procedures can be used.

Let us first show the Sales Ledger Menu from which we will select the various actions to take.

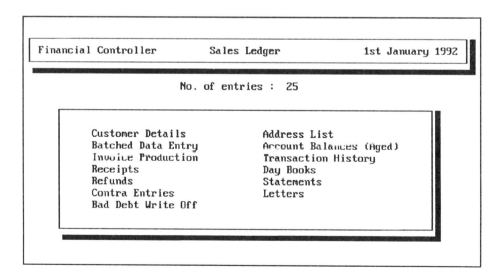

Figure 6.1: Sales Ledger Menu

And for comparison, we also show the Purchase Ledger Menu as well.

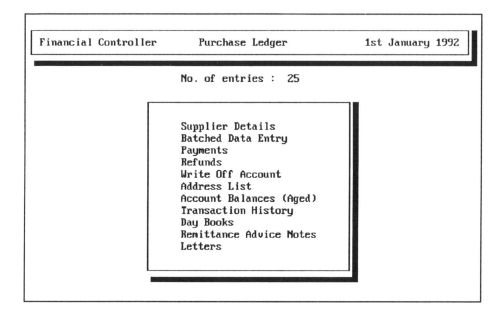

Figure 6.2: Purchase Ledger Menu

By this stage, you should now have entered all your opening balances, and all the names and addresses of current customers (as new customers are added, then use the Sales Ledger/Customer Details option from the menu, and proceed as described in the previous chapter).

Now we are going to deal with:

Entering invoices (we assume you are not using SAGE's own Invoicing procedure and subsequent automatic update of ledgers – see Chapter 7 for details).

Entering Credit Notes;

Receipts/Payments against invoices;

Returned/'bounced' cheques;

Refunds;

Contra entries;

Bad Debts;

Producing Reports and Analyses.

at the end of which you should be fully conversant with making entries into the Sales and Purchase Ledgers.

So let us start with:

Entering Invoices

Three procedures which it is recommended that you follow before starting entry are mentioned below. They represent good business practice and will 'trap' errors at an early stage. In practice, these steps are sometimes omitted by experienced users. However, we recommend that you endeavour to maintain the discipline involved since it can save you much time and effort both during and subsequent to data entry.

FIRSTLY: sort the invoices into date order (this is particularly important if you are going to use automatic allocation of payments (see later).

SECONDLY: as mentioned in the previous chapter, collect the invoices together into batches of twelve. Total these on an adding machine with a tally roll, and staple the roll to each batch.

THIRDLY: code each invoice with its Customer Account reference and Nominal Code at this stage (in fact, it is worthwhile investing in a rubber stamp like the one drawn below, which you can adapt to your own business, and can be used at all times).

INV NO.	DATE RECVD	GROSS TOTAL
DATE ENTD	ENTERED BY	AUDIT NO.
A/C REF	NOMINAL CD	PAID

Figure 6.3: Rubber stamp for Invoices

Now, choose Sales Ledger/Batched Data Entry/Sales Invoices. You will then be presented with this screen:

Figure 6.4: Sales Invoices Screen

With the invoice in front of you, you can now make entries. The information required is as follows:

A/c: (Account Reference) Enter this from the Invoice. If you have chosen the correct one it will be displayed in the box at the top left hand corner. If it does not correspond with anything known to the computer, a blue window will appear with a choice of alternatives which SAGE believes matches nearly what you have entered. If the correct one is there, move the cursor to it and hit [Enter], and the window will disappear leaving the correct entry in the 'A/c' space.

If you are not sure which is the correct code, then hit the [F4] key, which will again offer you the blue window, but with all the account references available. Choose the correct one and hit [Enter].

Date: Enter the invoice date here using a six digit number of the form: 010591 (meaning 1st May 1991). ALWAYS use six digits, and enter a leading zero if needed.

If the invoice date should be the current system date then hitting [F5] will automatically enter that for you.

Inv: (Invoice Number) You may enter any 6 character numeric or alphabetic reference here (from Version 4.2 onwards, hitting [Shift] and [F6] together on the second or subsequent line will increment the figure above by one; so if you sort the invoices numerically, this procedure will save time with the invoice number entries).

N/C: (Nominal Code) Here you must enter the correct Nominal Code for analysis. Again, SAGE will offer you alternatives if you have entered incorrectly, or [F4] will give you the full selection.

The Nominal Code will now appear in the second box in the top left corner for reference.

Dep: (Department) If you are using this, then enter the correct 3 digit code

Details: Here you have a 19 character field in which to enter details. This may simply be "Goods", or more detailed information like "Magnetic disks".

Nett Amnt: Enter here the Nett figure shown on the invoice.

However, there are two points to note:

> 1) if the invoice covers a number of items which have different Nominal Codes, then only enter here the Nett total for each item, and start a new line for subsequent items;

> 2) if you only have a Gross figure (including VAT) here, then enter it, and let SAGE calculate the correct Nett figure when we come to the 'Tax' entry shortly.

Tc: Here is where the VAT code is to be entered.

By default the following codes are used:

> T1: standard rate (currently 17.5%).

> T2: exempt items.

> T0: zero rated items.

> T9: non-VAT transactions (It should also be mentioned that if you are using T1 for the standard rate of tax, pressing the [F9] key will enter this for you, and acts as a 'short cut'.)

Tax Amnt: In view of the previous T/c entry the correct value of VAT should already be shown here. If it is not correct (due to rounding up or down on the source invoice) it is important that you over type with the correct value.

If, as mentioned above, you only have entered the Gross invoice value in the Nett column, now you should press the left shift and the [<] key and the system will work out the correct figures for you.

Complete each line as shown above, until you have completed all twelve on the screen. Check your tally roll total with the Batch Total on screen. Now press [ESC] and you will be offered: POST EDIT ABANDON.

A sample screen from ACE's transactions is reproduced below.

Figure 6.5: Sample Invoice Entry Screen

If all is in order, accept POST, and the ledgers will be updated.

If you need to make alterations, accept EDIT and you will retain this screen for changes to be made.

If you want to start the whole screen again, then accept ABANDON.

V 5 There is one important difference here with Version 5 when it concerns entries where you know only the TOTAL invoice value and not the amount of VAT.

In Version 5, on entering the 'Tc' (Tax Code) column, press the 'F10' key and the system will assume that the entry in the 'Nett Amount' field is in fact a Gross Amount and will calculate the correct figures for Nett, VAT and Gross values.

Don't forget also, that if, during the course of entering, you decide that you need a new Nominal Code or a new Sales Account Reference, you can do this 'on the fly' without exiting the procedure you are in.

In order that we might understand what is going on in SAGE when the files are updated let us just briefly deal with this point.

Updating/Posting Ledgers

With Sales Invoices, the following happens:

The Sales Ledger account for that customer is increased by the Gross value.

Debtors Control is DEBITED by the Gross Value.

The relevant Nominal Account is CREDITED by the Nett Value.

The Tax Control (VAT) is CREDITED by the VAT amount.

With the Purchase Invoices the entries made are:

Creditors Control CREDITED by the Gross value.

Nominal Account DEBITED by the Nett amount.

Tax Control DEBITED by Tax amount.

The entries which would be made on a manual system are shown below:

	DEBTORS		NOMINAL ACCOUNT		U.A.T.		BANK	
	DR	CR	DR	CR	DR	CR	DR	CR
Invoice	117.50			100.00		17.50		
Receipt		117.50					117.50	

Figure 6.6: Postings for Sales Invoices

Entering Credit Notes

To select, choose **Sales Ledger/Batched Data Entry/Credit Notes.** The data entry screen and method of entry is similar to the Invoices just discussed and you should proceed in the same way. The ledger updates are the reverse of the Invoice routines.

Receipts/Payments against Invoices

After having raised a Sales Invoice (or having received a Purchase Invoice) the next thing that usually happens is that a payment is received (or one made). So let's see how that is handled. The actual procedure in outline consists of a number of steps:

Calling up the "ledger card" for that account showing all outstanding invoices.

Entering details of the payment amount.

Allocating them against the relevant invoices (either letting SAGE do that automatically or doing that yourself).

Posting these entries.

Select **Sales Ledger/Receipts**. The following screen presents itself.

```
┌─────────────────────────────────────────────────────────────────────────┐
│  ┌──────────────────────────────────────────────────────────────────┐   │
│  │ Financial Controller          Receipts           28th January 1992│   │
│  └──────────────────────────────────────────────────────────────────┘   │
│                                                                          │
│   N/C Bank      : 1200           N/C Bank Name  : BANK CURRENT ACCOUNT    │
│   A/C Ref.      : JONES          A/C Name       : A Jones & Co Ltd        │
│   Payment Date  : 280192         Cheque Balance :       0.00             │
│   Cheque Number : 12345          Cheque Amount  :     499.38             │
│                                                                          │
│   Payment No. Tp  Date    Inv.      Details        Amount  Discount  Tc  │
│                                                                          │
│   FULL      1 SI 010192 12345  1 - Matrix Printer     0.00    0.00 T1    │
│             5 SI 010192 12349  1 - Printer Stand    233.83    0.00 T1    │
│             6 SI 010192 12349  1 - WP Software      411.25    0.00 T1    │
│             7 SI 010192 12349  6 - Ribbons            8.81    0.00 T1    │
│   FULL     10 SI 010192 12352  Advice in installtn    0.00    0.00 T1    │
│                                                                          │
│   Do you want to : Post Edit Abandon                                     │
└─────────────────────────────────────────────────────────────────────────┘
```

Figure 6.7: Sales Receipts Screen

Let us now describe the information which needs to be entered in these boxes:

N/C Bank: If you are only using one bank account, this will be shown in the box by default. If so, simply accept and hit [Enter]. If you are using more than one, then enter the one that applies to this transaction.

A/C Ref: Enter here the Account Code you have allocated to this customer (pressing [F4] will open the window with all of them listed if you are unable to remember), and the Account Name should appear in the box to the right.

Payment Date: The date the payment is made.

Cheque Number: Obtained direct from the payment cheque.

You will now be taken direct to:

Cheque Amount: Enter this here, which will then also appear in the Cheque Balance.

At this point, SAGE will take over and fill the screen underneath with the first ten outstanding transactions.

It will then ask the question:

`Method of Payment: Automatic Manual`

Before you make a decision on this, let us explain what will happen with each option:

Automatic Allocation: Starting with the earliest invoice entered it will pay invoices off in full, reducing the Cheque Balance by the relevant amount until this becomes ZERO, or there are no more invoices to pay. If it comes to an invoice whose value is greater than the Cheque Balance it will PART pay this invoice, and mark it accordingly.

You will then be returned to Manual mode.

Manual Allocation: This allows you to choose which invoices to pay off. In some cases there may be disputes about invoices, and payment is delayed so that some later invoices are paid first. In this instance you will need to choose Manual Allocation.

With Manual Allocation the procedure is as follows:

Move the cursor to the first invoice you want to pay off.

Hit the [Enter] key, and you will be offered the options:

FULL PART DISCOUNT CANCEL

These require some explanations:

Full: Selecting this will reduce the balance against this invoice to zero (and it will be wiped off the record after the next Month End reconfiguration).

Additionally the Cheque Balance will be reduced by this payment amount.

Part: There may be occasions where only part of an invoice is paid: maybe because there is a dispute on some of it, or you have agreed a part payment for some other reason. So select this option, and you will be asked to enter the amount of the part payment. The Invoice will be marked 'Part', and will continue to show in the system until fully paid. The Cheque Balance will be reduced by the part payment amount.

Discount: This is used when a settlement discount is being taken up. You will be asked to enter the amount of the discount. The system will then mark the invoice as fully paid and the discount allocated to the Discounts Nominal Code.

You will also be asked to give the Discount Tax Code.

The correct procedure when raising an invoice which offers a settlement discount is to work out the VAT on the offered discount whether or not it is taken up. Consequently no further action on VAT should be taken here, and the default tax code of T9 should be accepted. If for any reason the VAT needs to be altered, it should be done so by means of a Credit Note, not by using this routine.

Cancel: Use this if you wish to cancel what you have done so far in this allocation. The Cheque Balance will be returned to what it was.

Continue on in this way until the Cheque Balance is zero, or there are no more invoices to allocate. In this latter (unusual) case, when you try to escape, the system will warn you that there is money left on the cheque, and will post this to the 'Payments on Account' Nominal Code.

You may now proceed to post these payments.

Again to help us understand what is happening, let us see what occurs.

Posting payments

The Sales or Purchase Ledger account is reduced by the payment amount.

The Debtors Control is CREDITED by the payment amount.

The Bank Account is DEBITED by the payment amount.

Going back to our previous layout for postings of sales invoices (Figure 6.6), you will see how this payment affects the layout on the line "Receipt".

(In the Purchase Ledger it is the Creditors Control which is debited and the Bank Account credited).

Paying Off Credit Notes

When a Credit Note is posted to an account it is important to realise that SAGE does not automatically set this off against the correct invoice. You must do this manually.

The procedure is to select the above Payments routine, but to enter a ZERO cheque receipt. When the account screen appears, first go to the Credit Note and 'pay off' in full, which will result in the cheque amount being increased by that amount. Then go to the relevant invoice and use this cheque amount to pay off all or part of the amount outstanding.

Thereafter, the correct invoice balance will appear, or it will be deleted after a reconfiguration if totally cancelled.

Now let us see what happens when a cheque is 'bounced':

Returned Cheques/Refunds

Select **Sales Ledger/Refunds/Cancel Cheque**.

You will first be asked to enter the Account Reference which refers to the transaction.

You will then be presented with a screen showing all Receipts or Payments on Account for the current month.

Move the cursor to those which have been 'bounced' and hit [CR] for each one in turn.

When you have finished hit [ESC] and you will be asked:

Do you want to Post Edit Abandon Accept

'Post' if all is in order, or 'Edit' or 'Abandon' if not.

What happens if you accept 'Post' is:

'CANCELLED CHEQUE' is entered against the Audit Trail.

A new invoice is raised to correspond with the amount 'bounced'.

Journal entries between the Bank and Mispostings Account are made so that the Bank Balance is increased (for the Sales Ledger) correspondingly. (In the event that this is past Month End, you can follow the same procedure manually.)

Refunds

In this case, you should select the account reference required. You will then be presented with a screen showing all relevant invoices from which you may select the one for which the refund is to be made. SAGE then (a) posts a Credit Note to this account, (b) raises a new invoice to replace the one already paid off, and (c) posts Journals to the Mispostings and Bank accounts, marking them 'REFUND'.

Now we come to:

Contras

This situation can arise usually when you buy some goods or services from a supplier and he also buys goods or services from you. In such situations it can be agreed that instead of each of you writing out a cheque to settle accounts, you can both write off an equal amount from each other's debts. This is called a CONTRA ENTRY and SAGE can cope with the administration of this for you.

Please note: you will only be able to escape from this routine if the balances are equal, i.e. if the totals of Purchase and Sales Invoices to be allocated are equal. If they are not, then the difference will have to be allocated by a receipt or a payment. Make this entry first before proceeding to the Contra.

Choose **Sales Ledger/Contra Entries** and you will be asked for the Sales Account Reference and the Purchase Account Reference.

You will now be shown two screens side by side with Sales and Purchase ledgers on them. Work through the listed transactions and when the cursor is over the invoice to be allocated press [CR]. To move between the two windows press the [→] and the [←] keys.

Eventually, when all the Purchase and Sales Invoices have been allocated, the totals shown at the top should be the same.

If so, press [ESC] and select POST from the offered options. Otherwise select 'Edit' or 'Abandon'.

Bad Debts

Unfortunately, it is a fact of life that in most businesses today, bad debts occur. SAGE is able to cope with the transactions needed to deal with this situation by

(a) writing off the whole account i.e. if the customer has gone out of business etc. or

(b) writing off small amounts i.e. some outstanding invoices part paid where the balance is so small it is not worth bothering with, or

(c) writing off just one specific sales invoice.

Let's deal with each in turn.

Write Off an Account

Select **Sales Ledger/Bad Debts Write Off/Write off Account**. You are asked for the Account Reference, which you should enter. Then a listing will appear of all items outstanding on that account.

SAGE will then ask:

```
Do you want to write off all items?
```

If you do, select 'Yes'.

What then happens is that a Credit Note is posted to the Bad Debt nominal account but with a T9 Tax Code (You cannot just write off the VAT on a bad debt; there are special procedures about which your local VAT Office will give you advice).

Write off Small Outstanding Amounts

Select **Sales Ledger/Bad Debts/Write off small values**. You will then be asked for the maximum value to write off (must be less than £100).

SAGE will then list all the invoices that meet this qualification. Then, for each one, you will be asked to confirm whether or not you wish to write it off.

Press Y for Yes or N for No.

Finally, you will be asked if it is in order to proceed with the total write off. Say 'Yes' or 'No' as appropriate.

Write off specific Sales Invoices

Firstly, you need to know the Audit Trail (q.v.) number for this transaction. This can be obtained from the Audit Trail reports (Utilities/Audit Trail).

Select **Sales Ledger/Bad Debt Write Off/Write off Transaction**.

Enter the Audit Trail number when requested.

The screen will then show the Invoice details and ask you if you wish to proceed with the Write Off.

Select Yes or No as the case may be.

This now concludes the 'entry' part of the Sales Ledger, which constitutes the left hand side of the menu (or the first 7 entries of the Purchase Ledger menu). The right hand side consists of the reports which may be extracted from SAGE, which will be discussed in the following chapter.

7

INVOICING

Now let us spend some time on a most useful facility in SAGE – the Invoicing module.

With this you can:

> design an invoice just as you want to
>
> print out an invoice with the totals and VAT already calculated
>
> connect with the Stock Control module and produce invoices with unit prices already included (as well as automatic reduction of the stock balance as well)
>
> update the details directly to the Sales Ledger without further entry from you
>
> if you are using the Sales Order module you can also produce invoices directly from there

All of this can save much time and also reduce the possibility of entry errors.

To use this facility there are three distinct steps:

> 1. Pre-planning
> 2. Invoice Design
> 3. Invoice procedures

Let us deal with them one at a time.

Pre-planning

This step is a MUST. Skimp on time here and you will regret it! In fact it will probably cost you more time in the long run when you try to put right the things you have overlooked.

So you need to give serious thought at this stage to such matters as:

❏ will you use pre-printed stationery or plain un-printed?

❏ are you dealing with 'commodities' or 'services'

❏ what information MUST go on the invoice?

❏ what information would you LIKE on the invoice?

❏ where should everything go?

Another thing to think about is the type of invoice you will have. Within SAGE you can have a "stock" invoice or a "free design".

With the former you can call up the full description of the product, the unit price, the Nominal Code and the VAT rate from within SAGE. Additionally you can reduce the actual stock by the amount invoiced if you wish.

With the latter, you type all this information in at the time of production.

At first sight this would therefore mean that if you are offering a service (as opposed to a commodity) you could not use the Stock Invoice. However this may not necessarily be true. If you are offering a service which has a few standard descriptions and a fixed price, you may be able to still call them 'stock items' and thus save time by using a stock invoice.

To illustrate: let us say you are a firm of accountants who charge your clients by the hour. Within the stock control system you could set up a 'product' called, let us say: "Production of your Accounts". Then give it as unit cost your hourly rate; assign it a relevant Nominal Code and the correct VAT Code – and hey presto! Every time you produce an invoice you call up this stock item and everything is calculated for you.

IF you do (and can) work that way then initially you should go into Stock Control, set up your stock codes, and then 'put into stock' a large number of these 'units' – say 99,999, so that SAGE can take these 'from stock' when invoicing.

Now take either your existing invoice, or a large sheet of blank paper and plan out what the layout should be like.

To do so remember that in general:

each HORIZONTAL character will take up $1/10$"

each VERTICAL row will take up $1/6$"

(in both cases it is possible to set your printer to give different spacing (possibly $1/12$" horizontally and $1/8$" vertically) but for now we shall work on the above suppositions).

Also remember that when laying out "fields" (i.e. the space where information should be printed) you must allow for the TOTAL number SAGE assigns to that field e.g. a Stock Description line must allow for 30 characters.

If you are going to have the invoices pre-printed, it may be that your supplier can provide you with a pre-printed design grid which makes life easier all round.

Remember too – if you are unfamiliar with form design – that the total width of your form will depend on the capability of your printer first and foremost. Check your handbook first.

For instance if you have a dot-matrix printer it will probably only allow you to have a 'finished' form of about 8.5" wide (plus two $1/2$" tear off margins containing the sprocket holes). Wider printers can allow you to have say a 12.5" form, or whatever is specified.

As far as depth of form is concerned, plan to work in multiples of 1" (or 1/2" if you really must). Despite widespread metrication it is still essential that continuous forms are designed vertically in inches since the sprocket holes are standardised world-wide on $1/2$" centres. (The 'normal' invoice size commonly used in SAGE is 11" deep x 8.5" wide – 9.5" with sprocket margins)

It is also possible to use forms which have been 'partially' pre-printed i.e. they have the various boxes and columns pre-printed, but they allow you to put in your own information via the invoicing program. SAGE themselves can provide you with either partially or completely pre-printed forms.

Whatever your decision, it makes sense to consult with the company supplying you with forms first. Otherwise you may wind up designing a form which will cost a fortune to print!

So let us see how ACE design part of their invoice form:

```
************************************************
******            ACE SUPPLIES          ******
************************************************

              123  High Street              xxxxxxx
              Anytown
              Any County
              AB1 2CD

    Telephone:  01046 12 32 64
    VAT Reg. No: 123 456 789
```

xxxxxxxxxxxxxxxxxxxxxxxxxx	
xxxxxxxxxxxxxxxxxxxxxxxxxx	
xxxxxxxxxxxxxxxxxxxxxxxxxx	
xxxxxxxxxxxxxxxxxxxxxxxxxx	
xxxxxxxxxxxxxxxxxxxxxxxxxx	

Invoice No:	xxxxxx
Invoice Date:	xxxxxxxx
Order No.:	xxxxxx
Account No.:	xxxxxx

QUANTITY	DESCRIPTION	UNIT PRICE	TOTAL PRICE
xxxxxxxx	xxxxxxxxxxxxxxxxxxxxxxxxxxxxxxx xxxxxxxxxxxxxxxxxxxxxxxxxxxxxxx xxxxxxxxxxxxxxxxxxxxxxxxxxxxxxx	xxxxxxxx	xxxxxxxxxxx
xxxxxxxx	xxxxxxxxxxxxxxxxxxxxxxxxxxxxxxx xxxxxxxxxxxxxxxxxxxxxxxxxxxxxxx xxxxxxxxxxxxxxxxxxxxxxxxxxxxxxx	xxxxxxxx	xxxxxxxxxxx
xxxxxxxx	xxxxxxxxxxxxxxxxxxxxxxxxxxxxxxx xxxxxxxxxxxxxxxxxxxxxxxxxxxxxxx xxxxxxxxxxxxxxxxxxxxxxxxxxxxxxx	xxxxxxxx	xxxxxxxxxxx
xxxxxxxx	xxxxxxxxxxxxxxxxxxxxxxxxxxxxxxx xxxxxxxxxxxxxxxxxxxxxxxxxxxxxxx xxxxxxxxxxxxxxxxxxxxxxxxxxxxxxx	xxxxxxxx	xxxxxxxxxxx
xxxxxxxx	xxxxxxxxxxxxxxxxxxxxxxxxxxxxxxx xxxxxxxxxxxxxxxxxxxxxxxxxxxxxxx xxxxxxxxxxxxxxxxxxxxxxxxxxxxxxx	xxxxxxxx	xxxxxxxxxxx

	Nett Total	xxxxxxxxxxx
Delivered to:	VAT @ xxx %	xxxxxxxxxxx
xxxxxxxxxxxxxxxxxxxxxxxxxx	Carriage	xxxxxxxxxxx
xxxxxxxxxxxxxxxxxxxxxxxxxx xxxxxxxxxxxxxxxxxxxxxxxxxx	TOTAL TO PAY	xxxxxxxxxxx

A Settlement Discount of xxx % may be deducted if payment is made within xx
days of the above invoice date.
This amounts to a total deduction of xxxxxxxx if paid within this time.

Figure 7.1 Pre-Design of Invoices

Note how fields to be printed out by the printer are shown by 'x's; each x represents one character. You can easily see where (and if) the field fits in the available space, and where to draw lines and boxes (be careful to allow some space near rules to allow for variation in alignment – generally you should allow one character either side of vertical rules and half a row horizontally.

The sort of information which will need to go into the majority of invoices is:

❑ company name and address (if not pre-printed)

❑ VAT number (if not pre-printed)

❑ invoice number (SAGE can assign this for you consecutively)

❑ date (again SAGE can assign the current date for you)

❑ customer's order number/reference

❑ customer's name and address (will be extracted from Sales Ledger file)

❑ delivery address (if required)

❑ quantity of goods

❑ description of goods

❑ unit cost of goods

❑ total cost per item

❑ total invoice cost

❑ VAT total

❑ total amount to be paid

❑ discount for early payment etc (if offered)

❑ any other comments

So check very carefully first what information MUST go on, and what information you would LIKE to go on, and design the form to accommodate all of these.

Now – and only now – are you ready to start the Invoice design on the computer using the facilities within SAGE.

Invoice Design

Select **Utilities/Stationery Layouts/Invoices (Stock)** (or Free Text) and you will be offered the standard layout name ("invoice.lyt" for stock or "invtext.lyt" for free text). You may use this (which will simplify things later) and redesign it to your needs, or chose another name and design 'from scratch'. Using the standard layout may give you an approximate basis on which to work, modifying as necessary.

The design features for each type of invoice are broadly similar, so we will proceed on the basis of a stock invoice, but point out any differences from the free text layout when they occur.

After choosing or selecting a layout you will be given a screen which could look something like Figure 7.2 (this is the standard layout). Now we can begin designing (deleting all the previous information if nothing is relevant).

Two things to note before you start:

1. At the top of the screen you will see one box stating Line [??] and another Column [??] where the '??' show actual numbers. These figures tell you EXACTLY where you are on the form so that you may place your fields accurately.

   So Column 12 means that you are 12 positions (i.e. 12 x $^1/_{10}$") across from the left hand edge, and Line 6 means that you are 6 lines down (i.e. 6 x $^1/_6$") from the top of the form.

   Therefore if you first of all write the positions of the fields on your hand-drawn layout, when you come to place them on the screen you will be able to do with little trouble.

2. Also at the top right of the screen you will see a little box showing either [I] or [O]. This indicates whether you are in [I]nsert mode or [O]verwrite mode (the terms being used exactly as in word processing packages). This is very important to check otherwise you will either wind up typing over something you have already taken pains to get correct, or (and more likely and more frustrating) you will move all fields out of position as you put new information in place.

So start by putting the fixed, plain text you want printed out into position.

```
Filename : INVOICE.LYT     Line :    1  Column :    1 [I]  Memory (K):   290
```

```
*********************************************
******          SAGESOFT PLC        *******
*********************************************

    NEI HOUSE                              Inv/Crd
    REGENT CENTRE
    NEWCASTLE UPON TYNE   NE3 3DS
    Telephone: 091 213 1555
    Telex: 53623 SAGESL G
    VAT No.: 357 0469 41


                                                         Inv NoP
            Account Name
            Address Line #1                              Date#2
            Address Line #2
            Address Line #3                              Ord No
            Address Line #4
                                                         A/CRef


    QUANTITY           DETAILS           DISC  NETT PRICE      VAT

    Quantity          Stock Description   Dis % Nett Amount Tax Amount
                      Comment Line #1
                      Comment Line #2

    Quantity          Stock Description   Dis % Nett Amount Tax Amount
                      Comment Line #1
                      Comment Line #2

    Quantity          Stock Description   Dis % Nett Amount Tax Amount
                      Comment Line #1
                      Comment Line #2

    Quantity          Stock Description   Dis % Nett Amount Tax Amount
                      Comment Line #1
                      Comment Line #2

    Quantity          Stock Description   Dis % Nett Amount Tax Amount
                      Comment Line #1
                      Comment Line #2

    Quantity          Stock Description   Dis % Nett Amount Tax Amount
                      Comment Line #1
                      Comment Line #2

    Quantity          Stock Description   Dis % Nett Amount Tax Amount
                      Comment Line #1
                      Comment Line #2


                  Delivery Name                        Items Nett
            Delivery Address Line #1
            Delivery Address Line #2                   Total Tax
            Delivery Address Line #3
            Delivery Address Line #4       Carriage    Carriage

                  Notes Line #1                        Inv. Total
                  Notes Line #2
                  Notes Line #3
```

Figure 7.2 Standard Stock Invoice Layout

If you want to change the typeface a little you can introduce one or two printer control characters before the text in question (using the little blue window we shall talk about in a minute). The choices available to you in general are:

^O to start CONDENSED face print

^R to turn off CONDENSED print

^N to turn on EXPANDED face print – for one line only note!

^T to turn off EXPANDED face earlier than the end of the line

(you can also use a combination of CONDENSED and EXPANDED to give a BOLD type effect). But please check your printer handbook for the correct details for your printer.

(In the above, the ^ sign together with the relevant letter can be selected through the blue window).

So now we come to the part where we can insert fields from SAGE which will be printed with the variable information for each invoice. And this is where our "little blue window" comes in!

If you now press [F4] you will see a blue window to the right of the screen which can be scrolled through (using arrow keys or 'PgUp' or 'PgDn' keys) and gives you a selection of the information that may be entered into the invoice (including the ^ control characters mentioned above). By moving the horizonal marker bar to the relevant place and then pressing [CR], this information will be placed on the screen for you.

So what information is needed? The whole list and what they mean is printed in the SAGE manual, and will not be repeated here. However we detail the most commonly used ones and how they can be used, on the next page.

VARIABLE	WHAT IT MEANS	CHARACTERS
A/CRef	Customer Account Code	6
Account Name	Customer's Name	25
Address Line #1	Address information	25
Address L.#2,3,4	- as above -	25
Date#2	Date as 01/12/92	6
Inv/Crd	Prints either "INVOICE" or "CREDIT" at head	7
Inv No	Invoice Number	6
Stock Code	Stock Code	16
Stock Description	Stock Description	30
Comment Line #1	Additional comment lines	30
Quantity	Unit Quantity sold	8
Price	Sales price for item	8
Dis %	Discount percentage	5
Nett Amount	Nett Price after discount	11
Tc	Tax Code (per item)	2
Tax Amount	Tax amount (per item)	11
N/Code	Nominal Code	6
Line #1	Invoice description Free Text invoices	60
Line #2-9	As above	60
Carriage	Carriage value	11
Total Price	Total invoice price	11
Total Nett	Total invoice nett value	11
Total Tax	Total Invoice VAT	11
Inv.Total	Total to pay	11
Smt %	Settlement discount %	5
Sdy	Settlement discount days	3
Settle Amt	Total after settlement disc.	11
TotSettDisc	Amount of settlement disc.	11

... and so on.

So now start to place these in the positions they should be, as determined on your hand drawing. If you need to erase any boxes, place the cursor over the field and press [Del] and it will go.

One word of caution: make it a habit to **Save** the form every so often. Then if you make a subsequent mistake you can **Abandon** the form at that point and reload it at the last point at which you saved it – the writer has saved himself literally hours of time by so doing. (If you press [Esc] while in this screen it will give you the option of "Save Edit Abandon Print".)

Part of Ace's design looks like this:

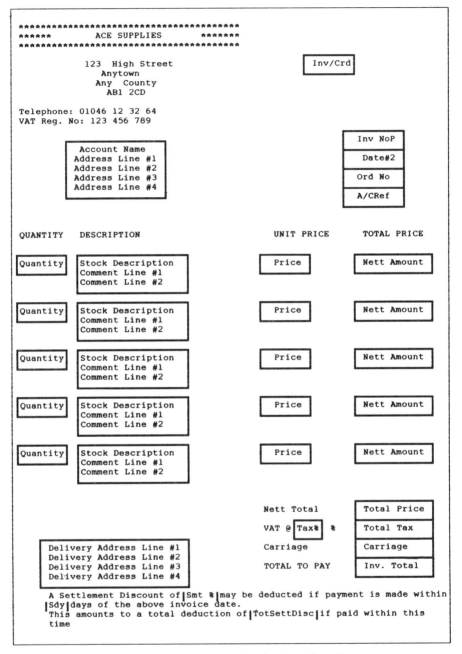

Figure 7.3 Invoice Design for Ace Supplies

(In the above diagram, field boxes are shown with double rules around them to make them stand out – they appear without these boxes but in a different colour on the screen)

It is worth mentioning that there are some 'free boxes' (Comment 1, 2 & 3) which can be used for text entry peculiar to each invoice, so you may place these where suitable on the form .

One more thing before you finish designing: press [PgDn] as many times as is needed until you can go no further to the bottom of the screen. Now -what figure appears in the "line" box? Is it the same as the depth of the form (in $1/6$")? For instance: if you have a 11" form does it show the last line as being 66? If so – all is OK. If not, then you need to either take lines out or put lines in (by using [CR] to give you blank lines) until this figure appears. The reason for this is that SAGE tells your printer when to jump to the next form on the last line; so if it is in the wrong place then the next form will start in the wrong place too!

Now, press [ESC] to get the little red box, and with a sample of your form loaded in your printer, select "Print". SAGE will then print out what you have just designed on the form. You should immediately be able to see if you have put everything in the right place!

If not – then it's 'back to the drawing board' to get everything where it should be!

Eventually all should be perfect, and you can save it for the final time; you can now use the Invoicing facility.

With free text invoices the procedure is exactly the same, but here the total price per line has to be put in at entry stage and cannot be calculated as you go. However if the correct Tax Code is put in it will calculate VAT and final totals for you.

Invoice procedures

Now we come across some differences between stock invoices and free text so we will deal with the separately.

Stock Invoices

Select **Sales Ledger/Invoices/Invoices Stock,** and the following page will appear on the screen.

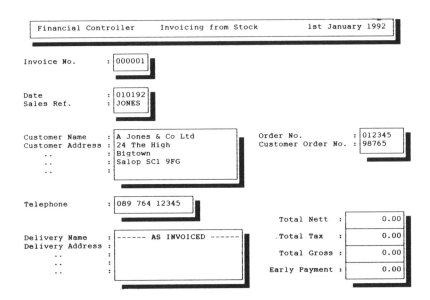

```
  Financial Controller      Invoicing from Stock        1st January 1992


Invoice No.        : 000001


Date               : 010192
Sales Ref.         : JONES


Customer Name      : A Jones & Co Ltd       Order No.          : 012345
Customer Address   : 24 The High            Customer Order No. : 98765
     ..            : Bigtown
     ..            : Salop SC1 9FG
     ..            :


Telephone          : 089 764 12345
                                             Total Nett   :        0.00
Delivery Name      : ------ AS INVOICED ------ Total Tax  :        0.00
Delivery Address   :
     ..            :                          Total Gross :        0.00
     ..            :
     ..            :                          Early Payment :      0.00
```

Figure 7.4 Page 1 of Stock Invoice Production

Now you must enter the relevant information. Included will be:

Invoice No: entered automatically by SAGE from the last entry (if you require leading zeros to be entered you must set this up in the Installation routine after escaping from SAGE). If you do not want to start from No. 1, enter the first number to begin with and SAGE will automatically increment from here in future.

Date: today's date being entered automatically by the system; adjust if necessary

Sales Ref.: this is the Customer Code; after entering this SAGE will put the full address details in for you. Over type if there are any significant changes to be made.

Delivery Name: add this as required. Otherwise allow "AS INVOICED" to stand

Delivery Address: as above

Order No: Any relevant reference you want there

Customer Order No: e.g. their Order No. etc

(The other information regarding prices is updated by SAGE as you proceed)

Having completed this page, press [CR], which will then show this screen:

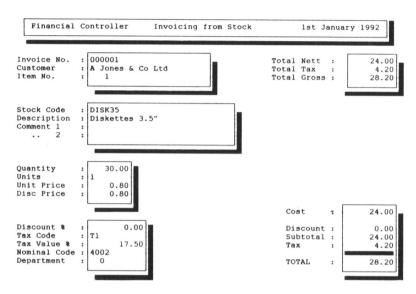

```
Financial Controller      Invoicing from Stock          1st January 1992

Invoice No.  : 000001                     Total Nett  :     24.00
Customer     : A Jones & Co Ltd           Total Tax   :      4.20
Item No.     :     1                      Total Gross :     28.20


Stock Code   : DISK35
Description  : Diskettes 3.5"
Comment 1    :
    ..   2   :


Quantity     :    30.00
Units        : 1
Unit Price   :     0.80
Disc Price   :     0.80
                                          Cost       :      24.00

Discount %   :        0.00                Discount :         0.00
Tax Code     : T1                         Subtotal :        24.00
Tax Value %  :       17.50                Tax      :         4.20
Nominal Code : 4002
Department   :     0                      TOTAL    :        28.20
```

Figure 7.5 Page 2 of Stock Invoice Production

Here you must enter all that is relevant.

For example:

> *Stock Code:* even if you don't print this out, it should be entered here to call up the description and price (pressing [F4] of course will give you a window listing those available if you cannot remember them all).
>
> *Description:* this will also be called up from your stock file and should be as you want. Alter if not.
>
> *Comment 1:* any 'tree' information you want to insert goes here
>
> *Comment 2 & 3:* as above
>
> *Quantity:* you must enter this manually
>
> *Units:* this should have been set up in Stock Control previously; ensure that it is suitable for your trade i.e. if the units are in fact hours and you invoice part hours, then the figure here must be,say, 0.25 (i.e. quarter hours)
>
> *Unit Price:* again as originally set up.

Discount %: if you have set up a standard discount rate in the customer record for this customer, then this will show here. If you have not, then the standard 'A' discount as set up in Stock Control will show here. Any of these defaults may be overwritten at this stage

Discount Price: calculated from the above

Tax Code: probably already set up by you in Stock Control

Tax Value %: calculated from Tax Code above

Nominal Code: should have already been set up in Stock Control

Department: as above

The other information on this page will be calculated by SAGE.

When you have finished this page, press [PgDn] and you will be offered a second page identical to the above for further stock item entries.

(If you should have more items than the invoice allows there are no problems since SAGE will print continuation sheets, numbering them 0001/A, 0001/B etc etc. and leaving the Gross totalling until the final page.)

After completing all items, pressing [PgDn] again will give you the final page which appears as follows:

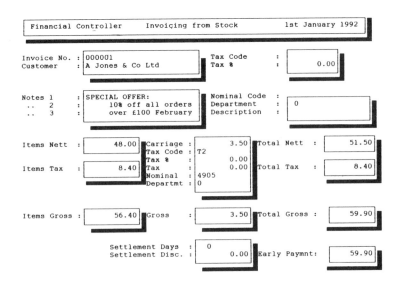

Fig. 7.6 Final Page Stock Invoice Production

Here the following may be entered as needed:

> *Notes 1:* Additional information you might want to include on the invoice (provided you have allowed room for it in your original design).
>
> *Notes 2 & 3:* As Note 1 above
>
> *Carriage:* an amount of relevant
>
> *Tax Code:* for carriage, if applicable
>
> *Nominal:* the Nominal Code for carriage
>
> *Settlement Days:* if you offer settlement discount, enter the number of days here.
>
> *Settlement Disc:* the amount (in percent) of such settlement discounts

Everything else is calculated automatically for you by SAGE and will show the total Nett and Gross value of the invoice.

Now press [Esc], and [Esc] again and you will be asked "Do you want to Save Edit Abandon", and assuming all is OK you will chose Save – which is posting only to the Invoice file. It is NOT posting to the ledgers at this stage.

The principle is essentially the same with Version 5 although the screens are a little different. For instance, the first screen appears as follows:

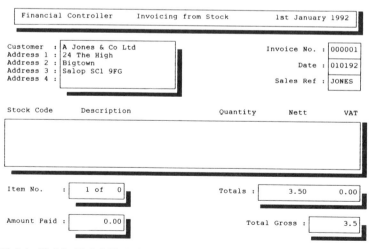

Figure 7.7 First Screen, Stock Invoice Version 5

The same information as above is required for entry here. However, when you are finished a second screen, as shown below, will pop up over the first one and will appear like this:

```
┌──────────────────────────────────────────────────────────────────┐
│ Financial Controller      Invoicing from Stock      1st January 1992 │
│ ▬▬▬▬▬▬▬▬▬▬▬▬▬▬▬▬▬▬▬▬▬▬▬▬▬▬▬▬▬▬▬▬▬▬▬▬▬▬▬▬▬▬▬▬▬▬▬▬▬▬▬▬▬▬  │
│  ┌──────────────────────────────────────────────────────────┐    │
│  │  Stock Code            : DISK35                           │    │
│  │  Description           : Diskettes 3.5"                   │    │
│  │  Comment1              :                                  │    │
│  │  Comment2              :                                  │    │
│  │ ─────────────────────────────────────────────────────────│    │
│  │  Quantity              :    30.00                         │    │
│  │  Unit Price            : 0.80        Units : 1            │    │
│  │  Discount %            :       10.00                      │    │
│  │  Tax Code              : T1          Tax % :      17.50   │    │
│  │  Nominal Code          : 4002                             │    │
│  │  Department            :   0                              │    │
│  │ ─────────────────────────────────────────────────────────│    │
│  │  Nett                  :       24.00 Disc  :      21.60   │    │
│  │  VAT                            3.78                       │    │
│  └──────────────────────────────────────────────────────────┘    │
└──────────────────────────────────────────────────────────────────┘
```

Figure 7.8 Second Screen, Stock Invoice Version 5

Enter the required information in the relevant boxes, and when completed you will be returned to the first screen with the first line having been filled in according to the information you have just entered.

Move to the second line if you have a second item, and press [CR] to be returned to the second screen for subsequent entries.

When all items have been entered press [F9], and the page shown in Figure 7.9 appears.

Again, the same information (with the exception of the Notes 1, 2 & 3) are allowable here.

Now let us look at Free Text invoicing.

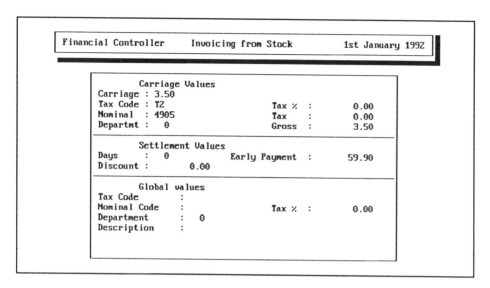

Figure 7.9 Footer Screen, Stock Invoice Version 5.

Free Text Invoicing

After selecting **Sales Ledger/Invoice Production/Invoices (Free Text)**, the same Page 1 as Stock Invoices (above) will appear. So that you may refer to it here in context we shall repeat that list of entries:

Invoice No: entered automatically by SAGE from the last entry (if you require leading zeros to be entered you must set this up in the Installation routine after escaping from SAGE). If you do not want to start from No. 1, enter the first number to begin with and SAGE will automatically increment from here in future.

Date: today's date being entered automatically by the system; adjust if necessary

Sales Ref.: this is the Customer Code; after entering this SAGE will put the full address details in for you. Over type if there are any significant changes to be made.

Delivery Name: add this as required. Otherwise allow "As Invoiced" to stand

Delivery Address: as above

Order No: Any relevant reference you want there

Customer Order No: e.g. their Order No. etc

(The other information regarding prices is updated by SAGE as you proceed)

Now press [CR] and the following page will appear:

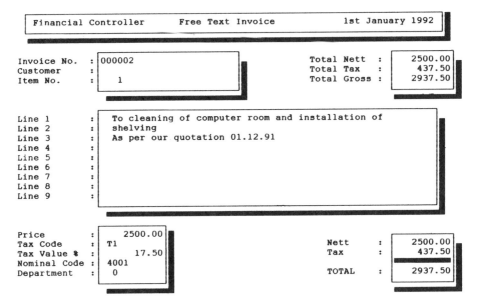

Figure 7.10 Page 2 Free Text Invoice Production

In Lines 1 to 9 (dependant on how many lines you have chosen to allow in the design) you can put the relevant descriptions.

The other information required is:

Price: the total nett price per item

Tax Code: the relevant VAT reference

Tax Value: SAGE will enter from Tax Code

Nominal Code: the relevant Nominal Code for the item above

Department: reference as required

The other information is updated automatically by SAGE.

Carry on to second and subsequent pages if required by pressing [PgDn].

(If you should have more items than the invoice allows there are no problems since SAGE will print continuation sheets, numbering them 0001/A, 0001/B etc etc. and leaving the Gross totalling until the final page.)

When all items have been entered press [PgDn] again, and you will have a page similar to that shown at Fig. 7.6 appear.

Here the following may be entered as needed:

> *Carriage:* an amount of relevant
>
> *Tax Code:* for carriage, if applicable
>
> *Nominal:* the Nominal Code for carriage
>
> *Settlement Days:* if you offer settlement discount, enter the number of days here.
>
> *Settlement Disc:* the amount (in percent) of such settlement discounts

Everything else is calculated automatically for you by SAGE and will show the total Nett and Gross value of the invoice.

Now press [Esc], and [Esc] again and you will be asked "Do you want to Save Edit Abandon", and assuming all is OK you will chose Save – which is posting only to the Invoice file. It is NOT posting to the ledgers at this stage.

Proceed in either of the above ways until you have made all the invoice entries you want, and then save them to file.

 The principle is essentially the same with Version 5 although the screens are a little different.

Please refer to the paragraphs on Version 5 above for Stock Invoices. The only difference is in the Page 2 screen, which for Free Text invoices looks like Figure 7.11.

A new feature introduced in Version 5 is 'skeleton' invoices.

If you have an invoice which is regularly produced with very minor changes from time to time, you can store this as a 'skeleton', then bring it back for the next occasion making any necessary changes then – SAGE will assign it the next available invoice number automatically.

When you have produced it for the first time, after completion press [F6] and you will be asked whether you want to 'Load Save or Delete' this invoice as a skeleton. Choosing Save will result in you being asked for a name (NEW.SKL is default) which you may select, using the .SKL as extension.

When recalling, you will be offered a list of available skeletons from a box which will appear. Select, load, amend and use!

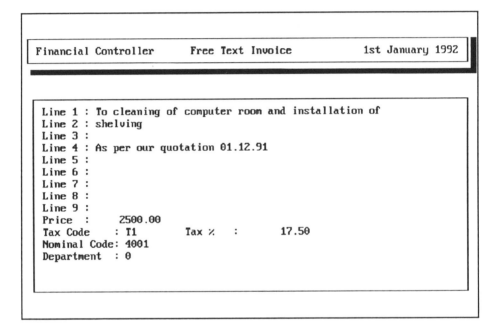

```
Financial Controller      Free Text Invoice           1st January 1992


    Line 1 : To cleaning of computer room and installation of
    Line 2 : shelving
    Line 3 :
    Line 4 : As per our quotation 01.12.91
    Line 5 :
    Line 6 :
    Line 7 :
    Line 8 :
    Line 9 :
    Price  :     2500.00
    Tax Code    : T1       Tax %  :          17.50
    Nominal Code: 4001
    Department  : 0
```

Figure 7.11 Second Screen, Free Text Invoices Version 5

Now we can proceed to

Invoice Printing

Select **Sales Ledger/Invoice Production/Print Invoices**

The following screen will then appear:

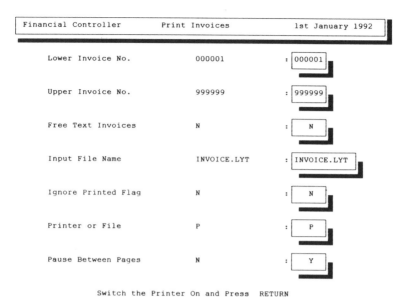

```
┌──────────────────────────────────────────────────────────────────────┐
│ Financial Controller        Print Invoices         1st January 1992   │
└──────────────────────────────────────────────────────────────────────┘

        Lower Invoice No.            000001          : 000001

        Upper Invoice No.            999999          : 999999

        Free Text Invoices           N              :   N

        Input File Name              INVOICE.LYT     : INVOICE.LYT

        Ignore Printed Flag          N              :   N

        Printer or File              P              :   P

        Pause Between Pages          N              :   Y
```

Switch the Printer On and Press RETURN

Figure 7.12 Print Invoice Screen

Let us proceed in order through this screen:

Lower Invoice No.: if you just want to select those that you want to print for some reason then you must enter the lower number here. Otherwise accept the default

Upper Invoice No.: as above

Free Text Invoices: if it is a stock invoice(s) you want to print then accept the default 'N' here; if free text, change to 'Y' for Yes.

Input File Name: The relevant STANDARD invoice layout will now appear here for the type of invoice you have chosen. Unless you have designed your own and called it something else, then you may accept the default here.

Ignore Printed Flag: this required a bit of explanation. When you print any invoice for the first time, it then sets a 'flag' in the program which says, in effect " this one has already been printed". So if you select 'N' at this point, it means that SAGE will only print those invoices which have not yet been printed at least once before. If you accept 'Y' then it will print ALL the invoices between the Upper and Lower Limits irrespective of whether they have been printed previously or not. This might be the case, for instance, if you changed something on the original invoice before you sent it out and wanted to reprint it.

You may not do this however once the invoice has been updated to the ledger. Any changes must be done via a Credit Note and/or new invoice.

Another situation that could arise is that if you are using a laser or inkjet printer you can only print a single sheet invoice at one time, and therefore you may need to have a second print run to produce your file or office copies.

Printer of File: usually P unless spooling for later printing

Pause Between Pages: if you are using continuous invoices then you can say 'N'; if using single sheets then say 'Y' so that SAGE will stop between invoices to enable you to reload.

Make sure the printer is switched on and on-line, and when you are ready your invoices will be printed out exactly as you require, with a high degree of professionalism.

Updating Ledgers

At some suitable time – dependant on your routines – you can have SAGE enter all the invoice information on the Sales Ledgers (avoiding the manual Invoice entering procedure mentioned in the chapter on Sales Ledger). This will include the date, invoice number, description, cost, VAT , and Nominal Code etc. – thus saving time and obviating error.

To do so, select: **Sales Ledger/Invoice Production/Update Ledgers.**

You will be asked for Upper Number, and Lower Number and whether you want to have a report sent to the printer or the file. Normally it would be best to send to the printer because then you will see if SAGE has been able to enter the information you set in it. For instance if you forgot to enter a Nominal Code or Tax Code, SAGE cannot update the ledgers and will say so in this report, So you can then pick out the relevant invoices, go back to Invoice Production, correct and update again.

Allow SAGE to print out this Update report and keep it with your month's records.

Display Index

From time to time, and certainly at month end, check that everything has been printed and updated by selecting "Display Index" from the Invoicing section. This will then show you which invoices have been printed and which updated to the ledger enabling you to complete that still to be done.

Of course there may be times when you may choose not to update at this time. For instance if you are keeping the ledgers open for a few days after month end, you may still need to print out new invoices for the following month. However until the prior month is closed you will not want to update these to the ledger. So you would take that into account.

Delete Invoices

And one final piece of housekeeping here is "Delete Invoices". This enables you to get rid of them from the files once they have ben printed and updated, assuming you have taken an office copy as well for reference. Enter "**Delete Invoices**" (be very careful if using the initial letter method when it comes to this section and the "Display Index" section as they both respond to an initial "D" with possible disastrous results if care is not exercised!). And enter the lower and upper invoice numbers that should be deleted. Later when in Utilities, you may care to go into Compress Data Files so that SAGE can reclaim the space previously occupied by these deleted invoices.

Credit Notes

The only thing we have not touched upon is the production of Credit Notes. However for all intents and purposes they may be assumed to be Stock Invoices when it comes to completion of the screen pages. Select **Sales Ledger/Invoice Production/Credit Notes** and proceed as above. On updating SAGE will make the entries in the correct ledgers with the correct postings.

Sales & Purchase Ledger Reports

We now come to the part of SAGE where it comes into its own, and you can start to control your business.

In the Ledger Reports for the Sales and Purchase Ledgers you can get full reports on:

Account Balances.

Aged Debtors/Creditors.

Transaction Histories for each account.

Daybook printouts – especially for auditors' purposes, but also useful in tracing queries.

Statements or Remittance Advices.

Debt Chasing Letters

Let us deal with each of these in turn, but before we do let us stress one point: if you follow our recommended procedures regarding Month End -especially about doing a Reconfiguration every month – then the procedures that follow are greatly simplified. You can virtually accept SAGE's default suggestions to proceed since there will be no duplication of information.

For the purposes of this book we are going to assume that you are doing this and our comments are made on that basis.. If your procedure should vary from this, then you will need to enter starting and finishing accounts and starting and finishing dates.

Account Balances

Generally we print out all outstanding balances, although the facility is there to do so within a selected range only.

Select Sales **Ledger/Account Balances (Aged)**

Unless you have any specific reason to do otherwise accept the defaults SAGE offers (see above), except when it comes to Display, Printer or File, where you will need to over type P or F if you wish to send to a printer or spool to disc.

You should then obtain a report like the following for 'ACE Supplies':

ACE SUPPLIES		Sales Ledger - Account Balances (Aged)							Date : 010292
									Page : 1
A/C	Account Name	Turnover	Credit Limit	Balance	Current	30 Days	60 Days	90 Days	Older
JONES	A Jones & Co Ltd	981.50	5000.00	653.89	0.00	653.89	0.00	0.00	0.00
	Alan Jones (089 764 12345)								
SMITH2	Smith Manufacturers Ltd	338.50	10000.00	397.74	0.00	397.74	0.00	0.00	0.00
	W Jones (081 3456 8965)								
SMITH3	Andrew Smith & Co	130.00	5000.00	152.75	0.00	152.75	0.00	0.00	0.00
	G Andrews (0438 234567 95)								
	Totals :	1450.00	20000.00	1204.38	0.00	1204.38	0.00	0.00	0.00

Figure 8.1: Aged Debtors Report

You now have a complete document to enable you to chase all outstanding debts at a very early time, and to know the situation in your business very accurately.

With Version 5 you are given the option of printing a 'Detailed' or a 'Summary' report.

The **Summary report** is basically as described above.

The **Detailed Report** shows each invoice or credit note individually, aged accordingly.

Additionally, when displaying this report on screen, you may scroll up or down through the total number of screens by pressing [PgUp] or [PgDn] respectively.

A further addition in Version 5 is for the Current Debtor's Control Balance to also be shown on screen (but not on the printed reports).

Additionally accounts who have exceeded their credit limits are signalled by means of an asterisk on this print out.

Transaction History

This is the computer equivalent of your original manual ledger cards.

Select **Sales Ledger/Transaction History.**

Accept the defaults (see above) and whatever report option (Display, Print or File) you want.

Additionally you have the option of deciding whether to have (as a printout) a new page for each new ledger account or not. Make your selection.

A typical report might look like this:

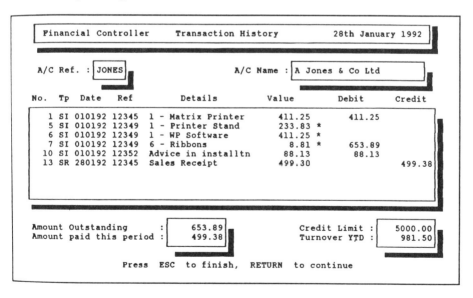

Figure 8.2: Transaction History report

The 'Tp' entry requires some explanation. This stands for the Transaction Type and will be one of the following:

SI   Sales Invoice   PI   Purchase Invoice
SC Sales Credit Note   PC Purchase Credit Note
SR Sales Receipt   PP Purchase Payment
SD Sales Discount   PD Purchase Discount
SA Payment on Account   PA Payment on Account

All outstanding unpaid invoices will be marked "*", and part payments "p".

 The layout of the Transaction History report screen is a little different in Version 5. The previous information at the foot is now moved to the head of the screen.

Now at the foot will appear an aged balance report for this account (note also that there is a provision for "future" amounts. These are for any invoices dated after the system date [which may not necessarily be the current date, of course]).

Further, pressing 'F10' will display the next account in the chosen range, and 'F9' the previous account.

If printing the Transaction History, you will find an extra column headed 'VR' (VAT Reconciliation).

This indicates whether the entry shown has been included in a VAT reconciliation.

Where this is the case, the symbol '-' appears, to show that it has been included in the VAT return.

If there is a 'V' symbol, then this indicates that it has been excluded from any reconciliations.

Daybooks

When we come to Month End procedures we will deal with the Daybooks as one of the essential printouts. To obtain, select all of SAGE's defaults, except for Printer of File options.

 With the Day Books print out, the same procedure as Transaction History (above) applies with regard to the 'VR' column.

Statements

It helps in chasing debts, and shows a great deal of professionalism, if you send out regular statements to your customers which show the state of their account with you. However, you will need pre-printed stationery for this, obtainable from a variety of sources (including SAGE themselves). Select Sales Ledger/Statements.

Here you will need to answer specific questions about the Upper and Lower references you want to include (or accept the defaults and send a statement to everyone).

When it comes to the question "Print Individual Items?" you have to make a decision. If you say 'yes' then each item on an invoice (if entered separately) will show on the Statement as a specific line too. If 'no', then each Invoice with the same reference is totalled and the words "Invoice" or "Goods" (depending on your earlier customisation) will be printed along with that total.

The answer to the question "Your Address on the Stationery?" depends on whether you are using Statements with your address already pre-printed, or whether stock forms are in use where your name has to be printed by SAGE.

The final option 'Message Lines' allows you print up to 3 lines of message at the bottom right hand corner of the statement.

 There are three changes in version 5 worthy of note:

1.You now have the option to use a 'free format' statement, i.e. one that you have designed yourself. To do this you must go to Utilities/Stationery Layouts/Statements.

2.The selection screen, in common with all others in Version 5, presents you with the default options specified in Company Preferences.

To change these, press 'C' (for 'Change') and move down to the fields you want to change, and over type as required.

3. One new option is shown as "B/Fwd Bal Up To".

This enables a line to appear on the Statement giving the balance brought forward as at the specified date.

Overdue Account Letters

This is a very useful routine that allows you to send a variety of letters to customers whose account with you is overdue. It is possible to design letters with varying degrees of severity according to the time overdue and to let SAGE sort out to which customers this applies.

Firstly you must design the respective letters using the 'Stationery Layout' in the 'Utilities' section. This is not within the scope of this book. For now, the information contained in the SAGE Manual will enable you to do this.

You may care to design three letters, calling them, say: ODUE1.LYT, ODUE2.LYT and ODUE3.LYT, using them as follows:

Select **Sales Ledger/Letters**.

Then, deal with the following questions:

Credit Limit Exceeded: If you have set up credit limits and wish to send letters only to those who have exceeded this, then choose 'Y', otherwise 'N'.

Zero Balances: It is highly unlikely that you would want to send a debt chasing letter to customers with zero balances. However, you may be using this facility to send some type of direct mail piece, in which case you would want to include all customers.

Select 'Y' or 'N' according to your needs.

No. of Days Outstanding: SAGE will send letters to only those customers whose time outstanding equals or exceeds the number of days you enter here.

This screen then clears and another appears. The following question should be answered:

Lower Account Reference: Normally accept defaults

Upper Account Reference: Normally accept defaults

Date of Report: This is the date from which all calculations of the overdue time are made.

Input filename: This will depend on which letter you will be sending. Choose such as ODUE1.LYT etc.

Printer or File: Either 'P' to print now, or 'F' to spool to disk.

Pause between Pages: If you are using sheets of paper (say letterheads etc) answer 'Y'. If you are using continuous stationery then 'N'.

Remittance Advice Notes

This will only apply to the Purchase Ledger and is normally sent with your payment to a supplier. The name and address box is placed so that it fits into a standard DL window envelope, and so can save time in writing or typing out envelopes.

Select: **Purchase Ledger/Remittance Advice Notes**.

Then proceed as for Statements (above).

The Nominal Ledger

We now come to the Nominal Ledger and the entries associated with it.

To recap: this ledger involves all transactions which are not on a credit basis, i.e which do not go through the Sales or Purchase Ledgers. They usually involve either cash or cheques, either inward or outward.

Additionally, we deal with Journal Entries, Recurring entries, Prepayments and Accruals, and Depreciation.

When entering the Nominal Ledger you will note that all entries are on the left hand side of the menu.

All reports are on the right.

Let us now proceed to:

Nominal Ledger Entries

Bank Payments/Receipts

(The routines are similar to each other, and so we deal with payments here; receipts are very similar).

Remember we are talking here about bank movements which do not go through the Sales or Purchase Ledgers. Select **Nominal Ledger/Bank Transactions/Bank Payments.**

The following screen will appear:

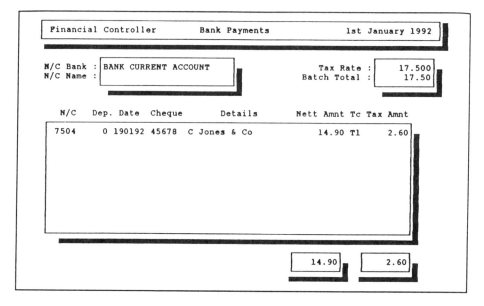

Figure 9.1: Bank Payments Screen

The following entries should be made:

N/C Bank: (Bank Nominal Account Reference). If you have only one Bank account then it will automatically appear here you only need hit [CR] to proceed. If using more than one select the correct one here.

N/C: (Nominal Account Code). Enter the correct code here. (Hitting [F4] will give you the full selection if you cannot remember). The full name will appear at the top left alongside "N/C Name:". Accept if correct.

Dep: Enter the department analysis code if you are using this facility

Date: Enter the payment date here (not forgetting the [F5] key to automatically enter the system date if appropriate).

Cheque: Enter here up to six alphanumeric characters for the cheque reference.

Details: You may use up to 19 characters to give a brief description of the payment.

Nett Amnt: Enter here the Nett amount (if known), the Gross amount if not.

Tc: Enter the tax code relevant to the transaction here e.g. T0, T1, T2, T9 etc. ([F9] enters T1 for you).

Tax Amnt: There should now be a figure in this column. If it is correct, then press [CR] to pass on to the next transaction. If not, either over type the correct amount, or, if you entered the Gross amount in the Nett column, press [left shift] and [<], and SAGE will automatically work out the correct Nett and Tax figures for you.

Proceed through the screen (using [F6] will duplicate the entry above, and Shift [F6] will increment any figures, say the cheque number, by one). Once you have reached the bottom of the screen, check the Batch Total with your tally roll and if all is OK, hit [ESC] to Post, Edit or Abandon.

Proceed until all entries have been made.

 In Version 5 the procedure for 'working back' a Gross invoice figure to a Nett value plus VAT is slightly different.

In this instance, enter the Gross Value in the 'Nett Amt' column, then, when in 'Tc' column, press [F10] key. The required calculations are then done automatically for you.

For your information, the following postings will be made by SAGE.

Bank Payments:

The Bank Account will be **credited** with the Gross amount.

The Nominal Account will be **debited** by the nett amount.

The Tax Account will be **debited** by the VAT amount.

This is represented in Figure 9.2.

	BANK		NOMINAL ACCOUNT		V.A.T.	
	DR	CR	DR	CR	DR	CR
Bank Payment		117.50	100.00		17.50	

Figure 9.2: Bank Payments

Bank Receipts:

The reverse of the above.

Cash Payments/Receipts

Select using **Nominal Ledger/Petty Cash Transaction/Cash Payments**. This operates in exactly the same way at the Cheque transactions above, except that you will not be asked for a Nominal Bank account reference.

Journal Entries

If you have a knowledge of book-keeping then you will understand the need for Journal entries.

If not, in brief let us explain that this is a means whereby transfers can be made between various Nominal Accounts without affecting the overall balances. It therefore is an unchangeable rule that the total of CREDIT entries in Journals should exactly equal the total of DEBIT entries. In fact, SAGE will not let you escape from Journals unless they are!

So why would you need Journal Entries?

Firstly: if you have posted an entry to the wrong Nominal Account, then this can be corrected.

> e.g. if £500 were debited to account 1000 when it should have been debited to 1001, then the Journal would consist of: £500 credited to 1000 and £500 debited to 1001.

Secondly: making payments, or deductions to certain control accounts e.g. wages, expenses, National Insurance, Tax etc.

Thirdly: as described earlier, to adjust opening Balances

Fourthly: month end adjustments for prepayments/accruals, etc (although there is a facility in SAGE for this to be done automatically for you).

And finally: from time to time there arises the need to transfer amounts between the Bank and Petty Cash accounts, which can only properly be done through Journal entries.

Select: **Nominal Ledger/Journal Entries.**

The information in Figure 9.3 appears.

Most entries, such as Date, Reference, N/C, Details, etc are as previously described for other procedures. However, a comment on the T/c (Tax Code) is required.

Most Journal Entries have no overall effect on VAT, so normally you would enter T9 here. However, any entries connected with VAT should have the appropriate T code entered here.

Enter the relevant details in either the Debit or Credit columns, and when completed (and with a ZERO balance showing), hit [ESC] to Post Edit Abandon, as usual.

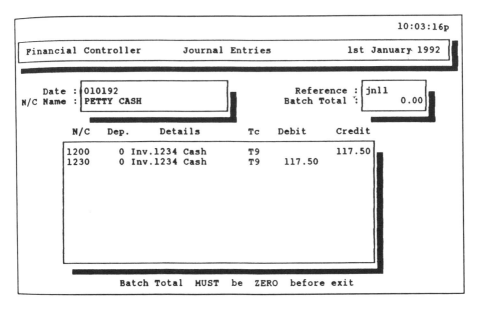

Figure 9.3: Journal Entry Screen

Recurring Entries

There will be certain entries which you will do every month e.g. standing orders on the bank for HP, Leasing etc. and certain Journal entries associated with these (see chapter on Special Procedures). Rather than make an entry every month, Recurring Entries enables you to set them up here, and then post them through the Month End Procedures routine when required.

Call up **Journal Entries/Recurring Entries**, and a screen will appear as shown in Figure 9.4.

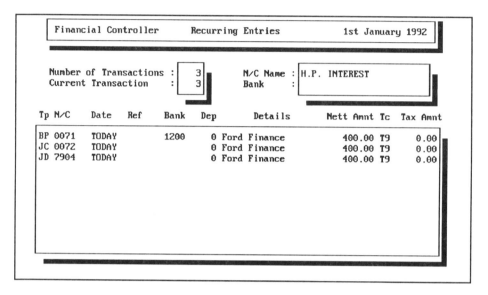

Figure 9.4: Recurring Entries

Most of the entries will be familiar to you, but the following require explanation:

Tp: The type of transaction required. This will only be: JC – Journal Credit, JD – Journal Debit, or BP – Bank Payment, since nothing else would be appropriate.

Date: You could go into this column each month and enter the appropriate date. However, if you enter "TODAY" in here (pressing [F5] will do that automatically), then it will enter the system date for you at the time of posting.

Otherwise, follow normal entry procedures.

When finished, hit [ESC] and select **Post Edit Abandon**

Please note: *accepting POST does NOT post these transactions to the Audit Trail etc. All you are posting is the information to a special Recurring Entry file. Posting will only take place when selected through the Month End Procedures.*

Prepayments & Accruals

These cover situations where (a) you pay in advance for certain services (e.g. rent) and need to allocate it in parts over the whole period it covers, rather than in one lump payment; and (b) where you get a bill for services which you have already had (e.g. telephone) and which it would be better to allocate in the months during which you used such services.

Let us deal with each of them in turn:

Prepayments

When the invoice for, say, the rent comes in, you would enter this as a Purchase Invoice in the normal way, and also enter the payment thereof as and when that occurs. This still continue to do. However, now proceed to: **Nominal Ledger/Prepayment & Accruals/Prepayment**.

You then have a data entry screen, which after completion (described ɔelow) looks like this:

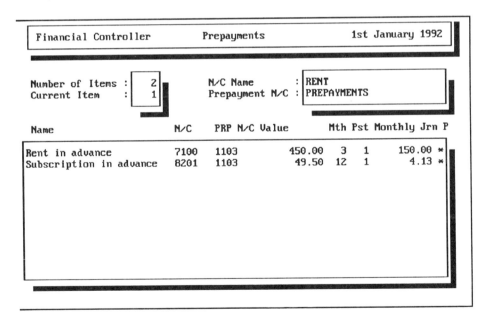

Figure 9.5: Prepayments Screen

The entries required are:

Name: Description of the entry.

N/C: The Nominal Account reference (same one as used when you made the Purchase Invoice entry earlier).

PRP N/C: This is the Prepayments nominal account. The default one is entered automatically, and you would normally accept this.

Value: Enter TOTAL amount of payment (excluding VAT) here.

Mth: Enter number of months over which to spread the entries (usually 3 or 12 dependent on item).

Pst: This is the number of months already posted – entered automatically by the system.

Monthly Jrn: The monthly amount to be entered – calculated by the system on the basis of the information entered above.

P: If a star appears here it denotes that the current month's entries have been posted.

When you have completed this screen, hit [Esc] and accept 'POST' as usual.

Important Note: this procedure has only set up the file to carry out these procedures. The actual posting only occurs when you select them from the 'Utilities/Month End' menu.

When postings are carried out, the following occurs:
1. A JOURNAL CREDIT is made of the FULL amount to the relevant Nominal Account – this has the effect of cancelling out the entry occasioned by the Purchase Invoice.
2. A corresponding JOURNAL DEBIT is made to the Prepayments Account
3. For this and subsequent months a JOURNAL DEBIT is made of the part of the allocation for that month to the Nominal Account, and a JOURNAL CREDIT to the Prepayments Account.

As a result, at the end of the period involved, the Prepayments Account will be reduced to ZERO and the Nominal Account for the service will have accumulated the amount paid in full.

Accruals

With Accruals, the full amount of the charge is not known until the end of the period, since no invoice is rendered until then. Therefore when selecting the Accruals screen for data entry, you must make a reasonable estimate of what it will be based on past experience. However, the system is such that by the end of the period an adjustment is automatically catered for so that the correct figures are produced.

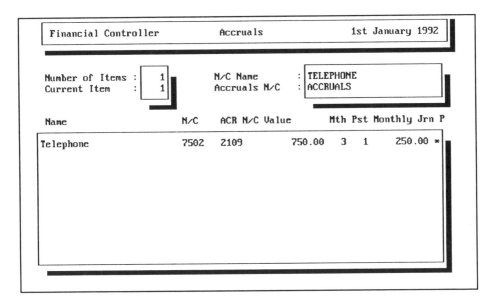

Figure 9.6: Accrual Entry Screen

All entries are as for Prepayments, with the exception that the Journal entries for the FULL amount are made by the system in the final month. Therefore, when the Purchase Invoice is received and posted the difference between that and the estimated figure will automatically be added or subtracted from the nominal account that refers to give an accurate result.

Important Note: this procedure has only set up the file to carry out these procedures. The actual posting only occurs when you select them from the 'Utilities/Month End' menu.

Depreciation

To give accurate results on your accounts, it is necessary to show the depreciation of Fixed Assets on a monthly basis. SAGE enables you to do this through the Depreciation routine.

Select **Nominal Ledger/Depreciation.**

The screen presented (shown with some entries) looks like this:

Figure 9.7: Depreciation Screen

The details required are as follows:

Name: A brief description of the entry

N/C: The Nominal Code (in the Fixed Assets – Balance Sheet) for the item being depreciated.

Value: The current value of the Asset

Tp: The type of depreciation required: it can be **S** for STRAIGHT LINE, **R** for REDUCING BALANCE, or **W** for WRITE OFF the whole amount with the next posting (if you are not sure which method to apply, again it is important to get some professional advice here).

%: This is the ANNUAL rate of depreciation you wish to apply to the calculations (often 25%).

Amnt: This is the monthly amount of depreciation, calculated from the foregoing information by SAGE.

Current: This is the remaining value of the asset after prior postings.

P: A star here will show that postings have been made for the current month.

When entries have been made, hit [ESC] and accept 'POST' as usual if all is in order.

When postings are made, the value of the asset is reduced by the appropriate amount and an equal figure is posted to 'Depreciation' in the Overheads section of the Profit & Loss account.

Important Note: this procedure has only set up the file to carry out these procedures. The actual posting only occurs when you select them from the 'Utilities/Month End' menu.

This completes the Entry side of the Nominal Ledger Screen. Let us now look at:

Nominal Ledger Reports

All reports have a number of things in common, which we will deal with here, extra information will dealt with under each heading.

Upper/Lower Account References: generally you should accept the defaults offered by SAGE. However, if you require specific information about one or a range of accounts, then enter their Nominal Code references here.

Upper/Lower Transaction No.: if you carry out a monthly reconfiguration, then you can accept the defaults offered. If you want specific information, then you must state the account codes here.

Date range from/to: Again, normally the defaults are accepted unless specific information relating to a named time period as required.

Display Printer or File: If you want to view on screen. select 'D' for Display. To print out, select 'P', or if you want to spool to disk for later printing, select 'D'.

Now let us deal with the specific reports in turn:

Accounts List

This gives a complete print out of all your Nominal Account Codes. We came across this when setting up our Nominal Account structure earlier.

Trial Balance

This is the 'heart' of the accounting functions. This gives a summary of all entries to all Nominal Accounts, and because of the double entry system MUST balance exactly (if otherwise, some data corruption has taken place -see chapter on Back-ups later).

Transaction History

This is a report of all the activity on each of the Nominal Accounts in entry order. Generally speaking you will need to do a full printout at every period end from here.

Control Account History

The Control Accounts are those special accounts reserved for posting the double entry to in this system. They consist of: Debtors Control, Creditors Control, Bank Accounts, Cash Account and Tax (VAT) Account. They are very useful figures to have to give you an idea of your liquidity and future obligations.

A full printout is usually conducted at period end.

 In Version 5 these are no longer shown separately (see below)

Day Books

This is a list by entry type of all transactions for the current period. Again a full printout is usually conducted each period end.

VAT Return Analysis

This requires some detailed explanation and is dealt with in depth in the Month End chapter later. For now, produce the listing for either time of invoicing or Cash Accounting procedures.

 Here, some major changes have been made. This we shall deal with in the Month End section.

Monthly Accounts

Again a detailed explanation is found in the Month End chapter. In essence this consists of entering the previous month's disk (no longer applies from Version 4.2 onwards) in order to obtain a current and cumulative Profit/Loss, and Balance Sheet printout as well as a Budget Report.

Asset Valuation Report/Consolidation

This is not within the scope of this book, and you should refer to the SAGE manual.

 There are three changes in Version 5 to the way these reports are dealt with:

1.You are presented with a screen showing the default options chosen in the Company Preferences selection. To override, press '**C**' (for 'Change') and then move to the relevant box and over type the required letter.

2.To move to the next account within the specified range on screen, press [F10] for the next and [F9] for the previous.

3.Control Accounts are no longer shown as separate reports. They may be selected as any other Nominal Account.

Additionally, there are two new reports available:

1.Bank Reconciliation

2.Bank Statement

As these affect the Month End routines, we shall deal with then in detail in that chapter.

This now covers the Nominal Ledger and allows us to now proceed to a the Utilities section.

10

Utilities

This section of SAGE can be called the 'housekeeping' part! It enables you to perform all sorts of actions to keep everything neat and tidy.

We shall cover the sections as they appear on the Menu under 'Utilities'.

First of all, here is the Utilities menu.

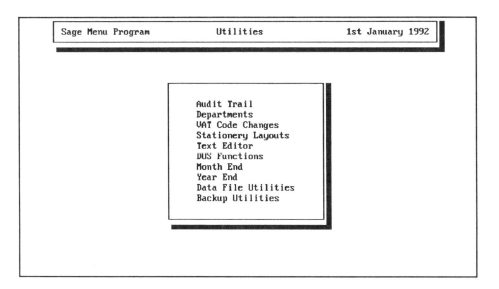

Figure 10.1: Utilities Menu

Audit Trail

This is a complete printout of all transactions that have been posted to the Ledgers. You may select all of the listing or a part, as required. It may viewed on the screen or printed out, according to preferences.

Herewith is a sample printout for 'ACE'.

```
ACE SUPPLIES                          Management Reports - Audit Trail                              Date : 010192
                                                                                                    Page :   1

No. Type A/C    N/C  Dep Details           Date   Inv.   Nett Amount Tax Amount TC Paid Date Cheque Amount Paid N-AC N-NC
----- --- ----- ----- --- ---------------- ------ ------ ----------- ---------- --- --- ------ ------ ----------- ----- ----
    1 SI JONES  4000  0 1 - Matrix Printer 010192 12345      350.00      61.25 T1  Y 280192 12345     411.25    5    5
    2 SI SMITH1 4002  0 25 - Disks         010192 12346        7.50       1.31 T1  Y 290192 98765       8.81   11    7
    3 SI SMITH2 4001  0 1 - Sage Fin. Contr 010192 12347     275.00      48.13 T1  N                    0.00    9    6
    4 SI SMITH3 4003  0 4 hrs Consultancy  010192 12348       80.00      14.00 T1  N                    0.00    8    8
    5 SI JONES  4000  0 1 - Printer Stand  010192 12349      199.00      34.83 T1  N                    0.00    6   11
    6 SI JONES  4001  0 1 - WP Software    010192 12349      350.00      61.25 T1  N                    0.00    7    0
    7 SI JONES  4002  0 6 - Ribbons        010192 12349        7.50       1.31 T1  N                    0.00   10    9
    8 SI SMITH3 4003  0 2.5 hrs Consultancy 010192 12350      50.00       8.75 T1  N                    0.00    0   10
    9 SI SMITH2 4002  0 5 bxs listing paper 010192 12351      56.00       9.80 T1  N                    0.00   12   12
   10 SI JONES  4003  0 Advice in installtn 010192 12352      75.00      13.13 T1  Y 280192 12345      88.13   13    0
   11 SI SMITH1 4000  0 1 - Laser Printer  010192 12353      895.00     156.63 T1  Y 290192 98765    1051.63   14    0
   12 SI SMITH2 4002  0 25 - Disks         010192 12354        7.50       1.31 T1  N                    0.00    0    0
   13 SR JONES  1200  0 Sales Receipt      280192 12345      499.38       0.00 T9  Y 280192 12345     499.38    0    0
   14 SR SMITH1 1200  0 Sales Receipt      290192 98765     1060.44       0.00 T9  Y 290192 98765    1060.44    0    0
   15 PI MAGSUP 5002  0 Supplies           020192 12345      250.00      43.75 T1  Y 020292 54673     293.75   19    0
   16 PI LANDLO 7100  0 Rent               030192            297.87      52.13 T1  N                    0.00    0    0
   17 PI ELECTR 7200  0 Electricity        050192 87654      298.52       0.00 T2  N                    0.00    0    0
   18 PI PRINTS 7500  0 Printing           130192 768594      16.71       2.92 T1  Y 020292 45678      19.63   20    0
   19 PP MAGSUP 1200  0 Purchase Payment   020292 54673      293.75       0.00 T9  Y 020292 54673     293.75    0    0
   20 PP PRINTS 1200  0 Purchase Payment   020292 45678       19.63       0.00 T9  Y 020292 45678      19.63    0    0
   21 CR        2399  0 Payment of petrol  020192             15.00       0.00 T9  Y 020192            15.00    0   22
   22 CR        2399  0 Payment of petrol  150192             15.00       0.00 T9  Y 150192            15.00    0    0
   23 CP        7300  0 Esso garage        020192             12.77       2.23 T1  Y 020192            15.00    0   24
   24 CP        7300  0 Esso garage        150192             12.77       2.23 T1  Y 150192            15.00    0    0
   25 BP 1200   7504  0 C Jones & Co       190192 45678       14.90       2.60 T1  Y 190192 45678      17.50    0    0
```

Figure 10.2: Audit Trail Print Out

Version 5 introduces some additional facilities to the Audit Trail. They are:

1.Selection of Ranges: you may now select a specified range of accounts (Sales, Purchase and Nominal) to display. Type 'C' (for Change) and over type in the respective boxes.

2.An additional column (VR) is shown to indicate whether an entry has been reconciled on a VAT return or not ('-' means it has; 'V' indicates that it has not).

3.The facility to scroll from the screen display both forwards and backwards has been introduced. Use [PgUp] or [PgDn].

Departments

This routine enables you to assign department references, as discussed earlier.

VAT Code Changes

It may be that the rate of VAT is changed during the course of a year. Select this function to do that.

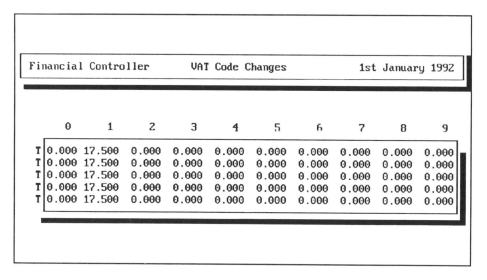

Figure 10.3: VAT Changes Screen

A screen is presented and you may over type the existing figures as necessary. It goes without saying that this should not be done during the course of the current month otherwise your VAT printout will have a mixed figure under T1. Leave until you have entered all transactions at the old rate before changing. If you prefer, a new Code reference may be assigned to the new rate.

Stationery Layouts

This is dealt with in Chapter 7 in the Invoicing section. Please refer.

Text Editor

This feature is not covered in this book.

DOS Functions

This facility enables you to perform certain Operating System procedures without leaving SAGE to so do. In particular you can EDIT, PRINT, COPY, DELETE, and change DIRECTORY.

Select: **Utilities/DOS Functions**. This screen then appears:

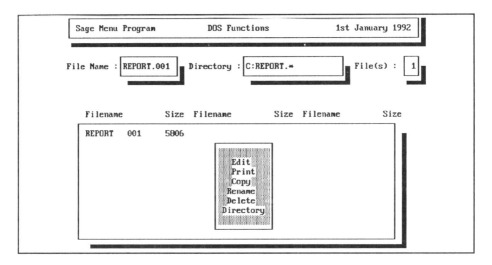

Figure 10.4: DOS Functions Screen

The following explanations apply:

File Name:the file currently selected for action

Directory: the directory currently selected. This can be changed when in the Functions menu (q.v.)

Files: the list of files meeting the Directory specification.

Hitting [CR] will now give you the DOS Functions menu. Moving the highlight bar to the respective line and hitting [CR] will cause the specific action to be performed on the designated file. Alternatively, pressing the initial letter of the required function will have the same result.

The functions are as follows:

Edit: This brings up the Text Editor, and enables you to modify the file as necessary. Hitting [ESC] thereafter gives you the SAVE EDIT ABANDON PRINT options:

Print: Enables the file to be printed. This is particularly useful to print out reports that you have previously spooled to file for later printing.

Copy: As the name implies, a file can be copied to a new one. Selecting this will cause the field "New Name" to appear, where you can enter such. Take care not to use an already existing name since this will cause the original to be overwritten.

Rename: Selecting this option again requests 'New Name' to be given. By so doing the original file is renamed.

Delete: Selecting this causes a message to appear: "Confirm deletion xxxx.xx" where 'xxxx.xx' is the chosen file. Select either YES or NO as appropriate.

Directory: Choosing this clears the current directory entry at the head of the screen and enables you to enter a new specification. In reality the entry should be viewed as a substitute for the MS-DOS 'DIR' command, and therefore you may use any of the legal DOS templates, including ? and *.

Month End

These routines actually post those entries you have made into the Nominal Ledger from the Recurring Entries, Prepayments & Accruals, Depreciation, and Stock Month End, all previously set up.

Select **Utilities/Month End** and then each procedure in turn that has previously been set up in the Nominal Ledger.

In each one you are given the option "Press ESC to finish, RETURN to continue".

If you select 'Continue' then postings will be made as previously specified and a printout of the action taken produced for either immediate printing or spooling, as usual.

Year End

We shall return to this subject in greater detail in a later chapter. For now we shall just explain what will happen.

All Profit & Loss Nominal balances are transferred to the 'Profit & Loss Reserves Account'. This is done by posting an opposite and equal amount to each of the accounts and posting the total Debit or Credit to the above Reserves account.

Thereafter a report of these actions is printed out or spooled.

Entries for the next year can then begin afresh.

Select by: **Utilities/Year End/Accounts** .

Data File Utilities

This covers 6 different features, described as follows:

Control Accounts

If we wish to add, change or delete some Control Accounts, you must FIRST ensure that a Nominal Account Code has been produced for it.

Thereafter, select **Utilities/Data File Utilities/Control Accounts.**

The screen showing the current Control Accounts with their Code numbers then appears. If you wish to change an existing code or put in one in an unassigned position, just type in the chosen Nominal Code. If you wish to delete one altogether, press the SPACE bar and then [CR].

```
Financial Controller       Control Accounts            1st January 1992


                Debtors' Control Account      : 1100
                Creditors' Control Account    : 2100
                Bank Account                  : 1200
                Bank Account Number 2         :
                Bank Account Number 3         :
                Bank Account Number 4         :
                Bank Account Number 5         :
                Cash Account                  : 1230
                Tax Control Account           : 2200
                Discount Account              : 4009


                Retained Profit & Loss Account : 3200
                Mispostings Account            : 9999
                Bad Debt Write Off Account     : 8100
                Depreciation Account           : 8000
                Prepayments Account            : 1103
                Accruals Account               : 2109
```

Figure 10.5: Control Account Screen.

Global Changes

This enables you to make specified changes to files globally.

The changes that can be made are specified as under and are represented on the first menu presented under this option: *Please ensure that you take a back-up before making these changes as they are irreversible once made.*

Ledger File Changes

The changes which can be made are:

Sales Turnover

Sales Credit Limit

Purchase Turnover

Purchase Credit Limit

Nominal Budgets.

Stock File Changes

The changes which can be made are:

Sales Price

Purchase Price

Re-Order Level

Re-Order Quantity

Discount A

Discount B

Discount C.

Type of Change

The type of change allowed is one of the following:

Add Amount

Subtract Amount

Multiply By

Divide By

Increase By %

Decrease By %

Give figure

Please note that with all of these, all the records in connection with the specified file are affected.

So, for example: If you wanted to increase all Sales Credit Limits by 10%, you would:

1. Select 'Ledger File Changes'

2. Select 'Sales Credit Limit'

3. Select 'Increase by%'

4. Enter 10 when asked 'Amount to Change by'.

Alternatively, to reset all Sales Turnover figures to Zero after a Year End:

1. Select 'Ledger File Changes'

2. Select 'Sales Turnover'

3. Select 'Decrease By %'

4. Enter 100 when asked for 'Amount to Change By'.

Posting Error Corrections

With the best will in the world, everyone makes mistakes from time to time. However, it is proper and correct accountancy practice not to allow alterations to entries previously made. In virtually all cases (except very minor payment date cases for instance) the correct procedure is to make the alterations by use of further Journal entries and any other double entry bookkeeping procedures.

To simplify this, SAGE has a Posting Error Correction facility which will carry out this procedure for you on current month entries. This takes two forms:

Reverse Posting — which has the effect of completely cancelling out the original entry enabling you to make a new, correct entry.

Correct Posting — where incorrect information (such as a Ledger code) has been entered.

SAGE makes the necessary Journal entries etc. to effect the correction.

In both cases it is essential to know the Audit Trail number of the incorrect entry. Obtain this from the Audit Trail under Utilities.

Reverse Posting

Select **Utilities/Data File Utilities/Posting Error Correction/Reverse Posting**

Enter the Audit Trail number when requested.

SAGE then states the procedure it will take, or will advise you what action you should take if it is unable to do so (for example, if the entry has been reconfigured last or in previous months).

You are then asked: 'Proceed with Correction?: NO YES' Choosing YES enables SAGE to do all the necessary postings.

Thereafter you must carry out the correct entry that you intended originally.

Please note: in the case of a Credit Note being raised to cancel out an invoice, the Credit will automatically be allocated to the relevant invoice.

Correct Posting

This allows for some fields that were incorrectly entered to be corrected. SAGE will let you know if your action is 'illegal'.

Select **Utilities/Data File Utilities/Posting Error Corrections/Correct Posting.** Enter the Audit Trail number when requested.

You will then be presented with a screen showing the details of the transaction. Using the cursor, move through the fields until you find the one that is incorrect (SAGE will not allow you to enter an 'illegal' field). Change the entry correspondingly, then hit [ESC].

SAGE will then ask: 'Do you wish to proceed and save the corrections? YES NO'. If Yes, then the necessary entries are made to affect the changes.

You are then asked: 'Proceed with Correction?: NO YES' Choosing YES enables SAGE to do all the necessary postings.

Data File Changes

This covers the three options:

Reconfiguration

This option in effect 'clears out' all irrelevant transactions e.g. invoices which have been fully paid, and 'one off' procedures. If this is not done, then the files get larger and larger and more and more difficult to manage. Additionally, when requesting reports, the defaults cannot be accepted but specified starting and finishing points have to be entered.

It is normally recommended that this is carried out as the final action in the Month End procedures.

To action:

1. Make two back-ups of your files.

2. Carry out all Month End printouts.

3. Select **Utilities/Data File Utilities/Data File Changes/Reconfiguration.**

4. You are then instructed:

```
Press ESC to finish, RETURN to continue.
```

With Version 5 a little more versatility is offered.

Firstly the system prompts you with the question: "Do you want to take a back up your data?" before proceeding, and if you say 'yes' will take you directly into the backup utility.

Secondly, you are asked to what date you want allocated and matched transactions removed. This gives you the option of retaining more than one month's transactions on file if you so wish. So enter here the last day up to which you want transactions removed. (In the case of a reconfigured Trial Balance you will have to choose the last day of the month you are finishing off here).

Resize Data Files

You may recall that when installing SAGE you were asked to specify the number of Sales, Purchase and Nominal accounts. After some time it may become apparent that you either chose too many or too few. This option lets you rectify that.

1. Take back-ups of your files.

2. Select Utilities/Data File Utilities/Resize Data Files.

3. Enter as indicated the new figures required to be initialized.

4. You are then asked:

`Do you have existing data: No Yes`

In this situation described above the answer to this question must be 'Yes'. Select this and proceed.

 (called Rebuild Data Files in Version 5)

Compress Data Files

This function applies to only: Stock Files, Invoice Files, Sales Order Files, and Purchase Order files.

With these it will search for deleted records in these files, and then rewrite the files without these in.

This is particularly valuable with the above files since they can become quite large and unwieldy in time.

 Version 5 introduces a new facility at this point:

Incomplete Transactions

This looks within the system to advise you of transactions and/or entries which are outstanding, or incomplete. This is the information it provides:

ORDER PROCESSING   unallocated orders
undespatched orders
orders to be invoiced
part delivered orders
stock overruns

INVOICING   unposted invoices
unprinted invoices

SALES LEDGER   credit notes (unallocated)
payments on account (unallocated)
part paid invoices
invoices over 60 days old

PURCHASE LEDGER   as Sales Ledger

Data Verification

This function has a number of options, but the only one that concerns us here is Accounts Data verification. This performs a number of checks on your entries and picks out errors of one form or another.

For instance it can identify:

Errors you have made in input: perhaps a payment date in advance of the system date for instance.

Internal errors: perhaps a Debtors Control which does not equal the total of Debtors for example.

Corrupt data, caused by a variety of factors.

Select **Utilities/Data File Utilities/Data Verification/ Accounts Data**. Normally, you would accept the default options offered next.

During the running of this procedure the errors are reported on screen and you asked to verify that SAGE should take the action it suggests. Alternatively, it will advise you of the action you can take to correct things.

After running through SAGE will have corrected the primary causes of the errors. However, there may be others still to correct, so it will ask:

`Do you want to run the DISK DOCTOR again: Y/N?`

Normally you would say 'Yes' to this.

This procedure is a very vital one in the running of a computerised accounting system and we would recommend that you run it at least once a day.

Back-up Utilities

In view of the importance of this matter we shall be devoting a whole chapter to the subject. However, we shall here describe the actual physical procedures for backing up, but our later chapter will go into the detail about the thinking and philosophy behind it.

The basic features of this are: at the end of a workings session the data files (*.DTA in the directory) are backed up onto a series of floppy disks.

These back-ups are not just copies of those original files, and are in a special 'back-up' format. The floppies used must be formatted by the DOS FORMAT command or equivalent. All versions before V 4.2 also require that the disks be empty of all prior data, which would normally require the DOS 'DELETE' command to be utilised first. From version 4.2 onwards this is not necessary, and if SAGE encounters a prior version of the file it is backing up it ask permission to delete if first.

If you are using multiple companies in Financial Controller then a separate set of disks should be used for each company.

SAGE keeps a log of the last ten back-ups made, and shows them on screen stating the Company, the day and the time of the back-up.

In the event of the necessity to use the back-up (say, for instance, some data has been corrupted), the RESTORE option is used within SAGE.

The back-up option is selected by Utilities/Back-up Utilities/Back-up Data Files/Accounts Date Files. You are then asked:

```
Do you want to BACK-UP your date files: YES NO
```

If YES is selected you will then be asked:

```
Which drive will contain the back-up files:
```

'A' will be shown as default. If this is correct, then enter [CR] to proceed.

As each disk is filled you will be asked to insert a new one. Do so until the back-up is complete.

'Restore' is virtually identical, with the same questions, and the same procedure, except, of course, that the floppies are used as the source to restore the files.

A great deal more needs to be said about back-ups, and so we will leave that until a later chapter.

| V 5 | This section is of particular importance to users of earlier versions of SAGE who have now upgraded to Version 5. |

There may be an occasion when you need to restore back ups of data files made prior to upgrading to Version 5. As the file formats are incompatible you will be unable to restore say, Version 4 backups from Version 5. So what can be done?

The procedure basically is this (assuming you have used the SAGE back up feature):

1. Take a back up of you data files before proceeding further.

2. Create a new directory – call it say "TEMP" (At C:> type **MD/TEMP**)

3. Into this directory install again your Version 4 of SAGE using the original disks. (Remember to afterwards go to the file SAGE.BAT in the root directory and alter it back so that typing "SAGE" does in fact lead you to the SAGE directory – the above procedure will have changed it to lead you to this new TEMP directory – it should read:

```
cd\sage
sage
```

4. Restore your old back ups into this directory (which is obviously compatible).

5. Exit this Version 4 of SAGE.

6. Go to the Version 5 directory and delete ALL files in the ACCDATA sub-directory (NOT just the data files).

7. Copy the files from the ACCDATA sub-directory of TEMP (the Version 4 directory) to the ACCDATA sub-directory of SAGE (the Version 5 directory).

8. Then run the MINDEX utility, which will convert the files to Version 5 format.

9. Load up the current Version of SAGE and take whatever action you want to on these old files.

10. When you have finished working on these files, restore your current files from the back up taken in Step 1 above.

To automate steps 6 to 9, you may create the following batch file in the TEMP directory:

(after typing "copy con trans.bat" then type

```
del c:\sage\company0\accdata\*.*
copy c:\temp\company0\accdata\*.* c:\sage\company0\accdata
cd\sage
mindex
sage
^z      (that is, Control key plus 'Z' key)
```

Then if you type "trans" after completing step 5, the necessary action will be taken for you (ensure you have altered the sage. bat file as discussed above, otherwise you will have real problems in running this!!).

File Import

This is a specialised feature which will allow you to import certain files from other programs in a compatible format. Refer to your manual for this operation.

11

Special Procedures

In this chapter we deal with the following special procedures:

Petty Cash and expenses;

Cash receipts/payments on Sales/Purchase ledger;

Wages and Salaries;

Hire and Lease Purchases;

Factoring;

Credit Cards used in business.

What happens if you change to VAT Cash Accounting.

Dealing with Proforma Accounts.

Petty Cash & Expenses

There are various types of transactions involved here, and the procedures for each can be carried out in a variety of ways. The following are suggestions.

Directors' Loans

Sometimes it may be that a Director puts money into the company which is used for purchases. In this instance, a normal Cheque receipt is made, posting it to the relevant Nominal Account for Directors' Loans (say 2103). When repaid, then a Cheque Payment is made to the same account.

However, a Director may sometimes use his own money to pay for some goods (usually Petty Cash items) and then request repayment. In this instance, it may be viewed that he has loaned the company the money for a period to purchase the items. Therefore:

Enter a CASH RECEIPT for the TOTAL amount of bills given using the T9 tax code since he cannot claim the VAT, and using the Director's Loan account Nominal Code (2103).

Enter a CASH PAYMENT for each of the items for which you have bills, assigning them the relevant Nominal Code for the item, and using the correct Tax code that applies, so that the company can claim the input tax.

When repaying, enter a BANK PAYMENT for the total amount, on 2103 Nominal Code and T9 tax code.

Therefore you will be able to see at any one time what liabilities the company has to the Directors.

(In the case of a Sole Trader or Partnership these figures apply to 'Capital Introduced' and 'Drawings' and are usually given separate nominal codes).

An alternative system used in some companies is to have a petty cash 'float' provided for approved employees, which is 'topped up' to the agreed figure on presentation of the bills every week or month.

In this case, set up various Petty Cash control accounts (either one in total, or one for each employee). Then for the initial float, make a JOURNAL entry, transferring the amount FROM the Bank (a credit entry) TO the Control Account you decide upon (a debit entry), using the T9 Tax Code. Every time you get receipts for expenses, enter as a JOURNAL, CREDITING the total amount to the Control Account(to reduce the value of the debt to the Company) , DEBITING the VAT exclusive amount to the correct Nominal Code for the purchase, and DEBITING the Tax Control account (2200) by the amount of VAT. Finally, when repaying or topping up the loan, make as a JOURNAL entry again as above.

Cash Receipts or Payments in Sales/Purchase Ledger

Occasionally you may receive some payments in cash instead of cheque. SAGE will not allow you to post this direct to the Petty Cash account, so this is what you must do:

> If you actually bank the full amount with other cheques, then it is simple: it can be treated as a cheque since it winds up in the Bank Account anyway.

However, if you do not do this and the cash is used for other purposes, then you must do the following:

> Post as a cheque payment in the normal way through the Sales or Purchase Ledger.
>
> In the Nominal ledger, make a Journal entry CREDITING the Bank Account (1200) and DEBITING the Cash Account (1230) with the amount in question (T9 tax code). This will then take it out of the Bank and into Cash.

Of course, if as a Sole Trader you actually do not bank the cash but use it for your own purposes, then you must also make an entry in CASH PAYMENTS to the 'drawings' account.

Alternatively, as a Director can only withdraw cash from the company as a) taxed wages or b) repayment of loans, if this cash is retained by a Director for personal use it must go through one or other of these procedures in addition.

This type of cash payment can so easily be overlooked and the longer it goes on, the harder it is to trace. It is important that a disciplined approach to such matters be adopted when computerising company accounts. It goes without saying that a similar, but reverse, procedure be adopted when dealing with cash settlements of Purchase Invoices.

Wages and Salaries

Here we have a situation where allowances have to be made for liabilities of PAYE tax and National Insurance, often paid at a later date than the wages.

The procedure we adopt is to allocate all the elements that go to make up the wages to various control accounts, and then to reduce these control accounts as payments are made. This way you can see at a glance where your liabilities are in these areas.

Make sure the following Control Accounts are set up (the figures in brackets are the default codes in the standard layout of accounts given by SAGE):

P.A.Y.E. (2210). + N.I.

National Insurance (2211).

Wages Control (none given, suggest 2220) 2230

Then proceed with the following JOURNAL entries:

NETT Wages (after deductions) CREDIT to 2220

Tax deducted CREDIT to 2210

N.I. (employers and employees) CREDIT to 2211

GROSS pay before deductions to DEBIT relevant Nominal Accounts (e.g. 7001, 7003, 7004 etc)

Employer's N.I. DEBIT to 7006.

(These figures MUST balance or else your calculations are wrong).

These steps are shown in Figure 11.1.

	DEBIT	CREDIT
Gross Wages	*	
EmployERS N.I.	*	
Income Tax		*
Total N.I.		*
Nett Wages		*

Figure 11.1: Postings for Wages

When you pay the wages, make a BANK PAYMENT to 2220.

When you pay National Insurance and PAYE tax, make a BANK PAYMENT to the relevant accounts (2210 and 2211).

In a theoretical situation, these control accounts should show Zero after making these payments, but in practice N.I. and PAYE is paid in arrears so these control accounts will show the Company's liability in this respect.

However, after paying out wages, always check the Wages control account (2220). If this is not Zero, you have either not paid someone (!) or your figures are in error somewhere. Check thoroughly at this point – do not leave it for later!.

Hire and Lease Purchases

There are two methods for carrying such transactions out. The first (which is the recommended procedure from SAGE) is the simplest. However, it really only works when you start the purchase contract during the running of SAGE i.e. not for prior contracts.

Additionally, it does not provide an on-going record of the amount of HP Interest remaining and/or paid, which is often of assistance to auditors.

Therefore the second suggestion takes these requirements into account.

A Simple system

Set up three new Nominal Accounts:

Car Asset account (in the Balance Sheet).

HP Agreement Account (Liability on the Balance Sheet).

HP Interest Account (in the Profit & Loss account).

Then make the following Journal Entries:

DEBIT Car Fixed Asset by value of car (the actual TOTAL value of the HP Agreement excluding interest)

CREDIT HP Agreement account with the same figure.

Then every month as payment is made enter a BANK PAYMENT split between the HP Agreement account and HP Interest account.

Let us assume that the car costs £8000, and that the monthly repayments are £400 plus £50 interest.

These entries could be summarised, as shown in Figure 11.2.

```
Initial Journal Entry of:
```

	DEBIT	CREDIT
Car Fixed Asset	8000	
Car HP Agreement		8000

```
Then BANK PAYMENTS each month:

                 Car HP Agreement       £ 400
                 Car HP Interest        £  50
```

Figure 11.2: Car HP Postings

Second system

Set up the following Balance Sheet accounts (one set for every agreement):

Car Account.

Car HP Account.

Car HP Interest Account

(and don't forget to adjust the layout of the Balance Sheet to take account of these).

Then set up the following Journal entries (if part way through a contract, then the up-to-date figures can be calculated and entered):

Car Account: DEBIT the actual capital value of the vehicle (NOT including HP interest).

Car HP Account: CREDIT the same, above, figure.

Car HP Interest Account: DEBIT the amount of HP Interest to be paid.

Car HP Account: CREDIT this same figure.

This results in the HP Account having both the capital account and the Interest amount included; and a separate record of the HP interest thus provided can also be helpful.

When making the DEPOSIT payment, make a BANK PAYMENT to the Car HP Account.

When making REPAYMENTS monthly, make the following entries:

1. BANK PAYMENT to Car HP Account of the TOTAL amount of the repayment.

2. JOURNAL ENTRIES of the INTEREST only as follows:

    CREDIT to HP Interest Account (Balance sheet)

    DEBIT to HP Interest (Profit & Loss)

This way, you have a very accurate record of your liabilities etc at any one time.

These stages are summarised in Figure 11.3.

```
When setting up accounts initially, carry out following JOURNALS:

                                     DEBIT           CREDIT

  Car Account                      Car Cost
                                                     Car Cost
  Car HP Account

  Car HP Interest Account          Interest
                                                     Interest
  Car HP Account


When making DEPOSIT for car:

    BANK PAYMENT to  Car HP Account

When making monthly REPAYMENTS:

    BANK PAYMENT to Car HP Account of TOTAL amount

    JOURNAL CREDIT to HP Interest Account (Balance Sheet) of INTEREST
    JOURNAL DEBIT  to HP Interest Account (Profit & Loss) of INTEREST
```

Figure 11.3: Car HP Entries

NOTE: in both cases, these suggested entries can be made using the Recurring Entries facility on SAGE.

Factoring

Increasingly, businesses are using the services of Factoring Companies to manage their cash-flow.

Typically, the Factoring Company takes over the Debtors of the client company. It will pay a percentage of the money due to the client company on receipt of their Sales Invoice and the remaining percentage, less their charges, when they are paid in full by the customer.

Understandably this can cause some problems in using SAGE unless handled properly. There follows a suggested procedure:

1. Create a new Control Account in the Nominal Ledger called FACTOR'S CONTROL.

2. Also create a new Nominal Account FACTOR'S CHARGES

3. Go to **Utilities/Control Accounts** and assign the new FACTOR'S CONTROL account as a Bank Control account

4. Assign the FACTOR'S CHARGES to a place in the Profit & Loss layout.

5. If you have some accounts which are factored and other which are not, go into **Sales Ledger/Sales Accounts** and type 'FACTORED' in the Analysis Field of those which are.

6. Produce invoices in the normal way and post to the relevant accounts

7. When money is received from the Factor, use **Nominal Postings/ Journal Entries**, to DEBIT the normal Bank Account and CREDIT the Factor's Control Account with the amount received.

8. When advised that the customer has paid the Factor, go into **Sales Receipts** and enter as normal nominating the Factor's Control as the Bank account.

9. Enter the Factor's charges as **Bank Payment**, Factor's Control as the Bank account and Factor's Charges as the Nominal analysis.

(It is important that you also reconcile the Factor's Control account at the end of the month in the same way that you do with the Bank Account (q.v.)).

Credit Cards

These can be used in business in a variety of ways.

For instance:

a) the Credit Card voucher could be presented to the Bank in settlement of your invoice

b) in settlement of a direct sale for which no Sales Account need be opened

c) the vouchers are sent to the Credit Card company, payment is sent to you and a handling charge is deducted.

Each procedure needs to be handled differently. Let us specify how:

Vouchers presented to Bank

1. Create a Nominal Code for Credit Card Fees (adjust the Profit & Loss layout to take account)

2. Allocate the payment to the relevant invoices using the Sales Receipt option

3. When you receive the statement from the Credit Card company you can process the charges as a Bank Payment in the Nominal Ledger and specify the nominal account for Credit Charges.

Direct Sales

Process Bank Receipt to the relevant Sales Nominal Code and when charged, process as Step 3 above.

Vouchers Sent to Credit Card Company

1. Create 2 Nominal Accounts: CREDIT CARD SUSPENSE (Current Assets section of Balance Sheet), and CREDIT CARD FEES (Profit & Loss Account)

2. If the original transaction was processed as a Sales Invoice, enter a CREDIT NOTE on the account and specify the Credit Card Suspense Nominal Account and a T9 Tax Code.

3. When payment is received from the Credit card company, process the following entries: e.g. if the original invoice was for £100, and you receive payment totalling £97.00:

Transaction	Nominal Account	Tax Cd.	AMOUNT
BANK PAYMENT	Credit Card Suspense	T9	97.00
JOURNAL DEBIT	Credit Card Fees	T9	3.00
JOURNAL CREDIT	Credit Card Suspense	T9	3.00

Figure 11.4

4. If, however, the voucher refers to a CASH SALE (and therefore the VAT has not yet been accounted for) the transaction should be entered as follows:

Transaction	Nominal Account	Tax Cd.	AMOUNT
JOURNAL DEBIT	Credit Card Suspense	T9	100.00
JOURNAL CREDIT	Cash Sale Account	T1	85.11
JOURNAL CREDIT	VAT Control Account	T1	14.89

Figure 11.5

And when the payment of £97.00 is received, process the following entries:

Transaction	Nominal Account	Tax Cd.	AMOUNT
BANK PAYMENT	Credit Card Suspense	T9	97.00
JOURNAL DEBIT	Credit Card Fees	T9	3.00
JOURNAL CREDIT	Credit Card Suspense	T9	3.00

Figure 11.6

Changing to VAT Cash Accounting

It may be that for a variety of reasons you decide to change to VAT Cash Accounting during the course of a year (you MUST have permission from the VAT office to do this – see their publications for the correct procedures and requirements). It is important that this change is carried out in the right way so that no problems are caused by the changeover.

The recommended procedure is as under:

1. Produce and reconcile your VAT returns at month end as usual.

2. Make the usual transfer by Journal from the VAT Control Account to the VAT liability account.

3. After the full Month End procedures, proceed to Reconfiguration as normal.

4. Exit SAGE

5. Within the SAGE subdirectory (cd\SAGE) type **INSTALL**

6. Select option (D) 'Edit Settings', then select option (I) 'Accounts Program Controls'. Select line (A), 'VAT Cash Accounting' and enter the first value as '1', and [CR] for the remaining lines.

7. Exit from the installation program ('X' at each of the prompts).

8. Reload SAGE, and select '**Utilities/VAT Code Changes**'.

9. Use the left arrow key to position the cursor over the first 'T' tax code and change this to 'S'. Press [ESC] to save these changes.

10. If using Stock Control, change the Tax Codes on Stock Items to 'S'.

You may now process new transactions under the VAT Cash Accounting Scheme.

When it now comes to VAT returns, you proceed as follows:

(a) Produce the VAT Return by PAYMENT for Tax Code 'S'.

(b) Use your Receipts and Payments Day Book from Sales, Purchase and Nominal Ledgers for reconciliation. In addition, use the following reports from Reports generator:

> TAXAP Tax Analysis by Payment
>
> VATIC Tax Analysis Invoices & Credit Management
>
> VATPR Tax Analysis Payments & Receipts reports.

Dealing with Proforma Accounts

Some companies use a Proforma Invoice as a means of asking for payment before goods are despatched. To deal with this type of transaction proceed as under:

1. Create a Sales Ledger Account called 'Proforma'.

2. When the invoice is raised to the customer *do not enter on the ledger* at this stage.

3. When the PAYMENT is received, enter a SALES RECEIPT to the 'Proforma' account as a 'Payment on Account'

4. When the goods are despatched, enter the Sales Invoice to the 'Proforma' account.

5. Allocate the Payment on Account to the relevant invoice as follows:
   a) Select Sales Receipt
   b) Enter a cheque value of £ 0.00
   c) Select Manual Allocation
   d) Pick up the Payment on Account and allocate in FULL
   e) Pay off the Invoice in FULL from the accumulated value from step d) above.

This routine works for both the Sales and the Purchase Ledgers.

The above covers a few of the situations that can arise in many businesses.

Doubtless you may think of others. If you use the principles outlined above you should be able to arrive at a satisfactory solution. We recommend that you first set down the transactions as balancing Debits and Credits to the various Nominal Accounts. Then see what the ultimate result is. If it is what you want – then you've probably got it right. If not – try again.

But, as always, if you are not sure, ask your Accountant how he would like it done! The important thing to remember is this: make sure that you print out every month the recommended reports (see relevant chapter). Then if you have made a mistake, at least your Accountant can trace what you have done and make adjustments as necessary.

12

Back-up Procedures

We now come to the subject which you have probably already realised, the writer considers to be one of the most important in the book.

Why? It can best be answered by comparing it to house insurance. Most of the time you never need it, but when you do, you're glad you had it! After a short while your business will become totally dependant on your computerised accounting system – you'll wonder how you ever managed without it – until the day you have to manage without it! THEN you will be glad you took back-ups.

Let us consider for a moment what could cause such a situation.

❏ Your computer 'goes down' in the middle of work.

❏ Perhaps there is a power failure or some other such problem right in the middle of you using SAGE. In such a situation there is a good possibility that your data files will be corrupted i.e. SAGE will no longer be able to read them when you start up again. Then what? If you have a back-up – no problem. If you don't – then you really do have a serious problem.

❏ A virus gets into your system! This may be unlikely if you are using proprietary software and can trust everyone. If not, then file corruption can occur with the same problems as above.

❏ The accounts computer just won't start today! With back-ups and copies of the SAGE program you can transfer to another computer for the time being without any delay.

❏ You (or your operators) have made a lot of errors. Let us say, for instance, that you selected Bank Receipts when it should have been Bank Payments, and you have made several hundred entries incorrectly. You could reverse them all and start again. But it is a lot quicker if you could return to the last back-up and start all over again, correctly this time.

In all these situations (with the exception of the last) think about the consequences if you haven't taken back-ups:

Who owes you money? How will you chase it up?.

To whom do you owe money? Can you be certain their Statement is correct?

How much should you pay the VAT? What happens if you make an error, even unintentionally? What is the current fine for that?

How will you do your end of year accounts and tax returns? What are the consequences of that? How much will failure to do so cost you?

Could your business survive loss of all your data?

....and so on. The list is frightening.

When you thus consider the consequences, you maybe can now see why we stress the habit of regular back-ups.

Good Habits

Every time you try to exit from SAGE the question is posed: "Do you want to back-up your data?"

WE WOULD RECOMMEND THAT YOU ALWAYS ANSWER 'YES' TO THAT!

We are going to discuss several regimes that you can introduce for a proper schedule of back-ups – but if you were only to do the above every time you exited, it would doubtless cover a high percentage of the eventualities previously mentioned.

We would certainly recommend that you ALWAYS have by you a diskette labelled "Interim" that you back-up to every time you exit from SAGE.

However, let us now discuss several regimes for back-up routines. The one you choose depends to an extent on the amount of data you input and the degree of 'safety' you wish to achieve.

Minimum Recommendations

Have a set of disks labelled thus:

Friday 1 (or F1 if you prefer)

Monday (M)

Tuesday (Tu)

Wednesday (W)

Thursday (Th)

Friday 2 (F2) (assuming you work a five day week)

Start your routine at the close of business on a Friday, and back-up to Friday 1. Every subsequent weekday, use the fitting back-up disk(s) until the Friday when you should use Friday 2. Next week, use the Monday to Thursday disk(s) again, and then Friday 1 again.

Thus you will readily see that before the Friday back-up you actually have an archive which is two weeks old, and the newest 1 day old. So you may restore for any time during that period.

Ultimate Protection

The following suggestion will give you a minimum three months of archived data and give a very high level of disaster protection.

The regime starts off exactly as the 'minimum recommendations' (above). But then on the third Friday you would use another set of disks called "Friday 3".

Then on the fourth Friday use "Month 1". Thereafter use "Month 2" and "Month 3" at successive fourth Fridays. On Month 4 you would re-use Month 1's disks.

Naturally to keep track of these it is important to keep some sort of log so that you know exactly where you are and where the back-ups have been made. Note that this requires ten sets of disks which is probably a small investment to make for such a high degree of protection.

Additional Comments

Apart from the above suggestions, ensure that you produce TWO copies of the End of Month files – either as a COPY if you are using a copy of SAGE before Version 4.2., or as back-ups afterwards. And keep these copies indefinitely, certainly for as long as you are legally required to retain all physical records (which is six years at the time of writing). Keep one copy in the building (preferably in a fire-proof safe), and the other in an off-site location.

The Problems

Doubtless you can see for yourself how valuable such a regime would be PROVIDED IT IS ACTUALLY IMPLEMENTED! And that is where the problem comes in. Whilst every one agrees in principle with the policy, in the rush to get work done before the end of the day usually there is little time left to do the back-ups, and the tendency is to say: "it won't hurt to miss it this time – I'll make sure I do it tomorrow." Murphy's Law being what it is, you can be sure that that is the day you will have problems! So don't miss a single day of back-ups if you value your peace of mind.

This really is where good management comes into play.

Will you ensure and control the carrying out of back-ups? Will you insist on a log being kept? Will you introduce relevant disciplines when it does not happen as instructed? Remember: the future of your company is at stake here – it is not something to be treated lightly!.

13

Month and Year End Procedures

Now we come to the part where all your efforts bear fruit and give you results. You will see the records printed out that enable you to monitor and control the progress of your company.

Again it is important that good disciplines and methods are introduced right from the beginning so that nothing is missed.

What follows is a suggested 'order of events' which will guarantee that you miss nothing and keep things in good order.

In outline what we shall do is:

1. Post all Depreciations, Prepayment and Accruals, and Recurring Entries.

2. Make an initial back-up of data.

3. Verify the integrity of the data.

4. Make some checks that nothing has been overlooked.

5. Print out all the necessary reports.

6. Produce Profit & Loss and Budget reports.

7. Produce Statements and Remittance Advices.

8. Reconfigure in preparation for the new month.

So let's take each of these steps in turn, and then we will finish by giving the information again in the form of a check list which you may use.

Update Data

You will recall that we set up various Monthly files: Recurring Entries, Prepayments and Accruals , and Depreciation. Now we need to post them to the ledgers.

First, therefore, go the relevant sections in the Nominal Ledger and make alterations to dates if this is needed (if you use the TODAY method it will make the entry for the system date).

Now select **Utilities/ Month End** and then action the relevant sections as appropriate, which results in them being posted as previously decided.

Initial Back-up

This is important so that if anything goes wrong in the following steps we can at least restore and start all over again.

Select **Utilities/Back-up Utilities** and proceed as outlined previously.

Verify the Integrity of the Data

This step is essential. There is no point in proceeding any further until this has been carried out since you could be working on incorrect or corrupt data.

Select **Utilities/Data File Utilities/Data Verification** and proceed as previously discussed.

If there are problems here then let Disk Doctor put them right, or if there is corruption, return to the last verified back-up.

Only when everything is in order here can we proceed to the next action, which is:

Various Checks

We must now take some printouts and do some checks in connection with them.

Bank Record

Select **Nominal Ledger/Control Accounts Reports/Bank Accounts** and printout as report for each of the accounts.

Now you must verify everything with the Bank Statement which we assume you receive every month (if not, insist on one from now on!).

What you need to do is to check that every entry on the Statement has been made to the computer and that the balances all agree.

However, it is highly unlikely that the Statement will be 100% up to date with the computer since there may well be cheques you have issued and money you have received which has been entered into the computer but not yet appeared on the Bank Statement. Therefore it is necessary to 'adjust' your figures to allow for that.

In Appendix 1 you will find a sample of a form which will enable you to control that. Feel free either to photocopy it, or reproduce it yourself for your use.

To explain:

Start by entering the last final balance on your Bank Statement (and draw a line underneath it so you know your point of action).

Then, list all cheques which have gone on to the computer but which do not appear on the Statement.

DEDUCT these from the Balance.

Then list all receipts which have gone on to the computer but do not yet appear on the Statement.

ADD these to the Balance.

The figure you thus obtain we call the 'Adjusted Statement Balance.' Then write down the Balance which appears on your Bank Account report.

The two should be identical. If they are not, then you MUST start looking for the reason before you proceed further.

Look first at what the difference is — that may give you a clue as to where the problem is as it may be a figure you recognize. Maybe you have overlooked a Standing Order or a direct debit.

Have any cheques been issued and then cancelled? Have any 'bounced'? Have you made an incorrect entry of the amount? And so on.

It cannot be stressed too much that you should not proceed beyond this point until the two balances correspond exactly. If they do not, there is an error, and that must be found before you can do anything else. Indeed, what we have said here also applies to the Factor's Account if you are using that arrangement.

 With Version 5 an improved method of checking the Bank Account is offered, wherein this can be done 'on screen' as it were.

Select: **Nominal Ledger/Bank Reconciliation** and a screen like the following will appear:

Figure 13.1 Bank Reconciliation Screen

Also have before you the latest copy of your bank statement.

On the screen, the following explanations are appropriate:

B/Fwd Balance: This is the reconciled, agreed figure brought forward from the last reconciliation (which should be the same as the opening balance on your bank statement)

Trial Balance: This is the up to date figure from the program, taking account of all entries you have made in or out – the figure against which we have to reconcile matters.

Statement Balance: The final balance on your statement, adjusted as each reconciliation is made. When you have finished, this must be the same as that appearing on your bank statement, otherwise an error has been made.

Uncleared Items: A summary of outstanding items presently unreconciled. This figure is reduced as lines are reconciled.

To proceed with the reconciliation process: as you locate each item on your bank statement, try to find the corresponding entry on the screen. If you do, mover the cursor to it and then press [Enter], and it will be highlighted in a different colour (the statement balance and uncleared items boxes will be adjusted automatically).

If, as you proceed, you find items appearing on the statement but not on screen (say, for instance, a bank charge, interest charge, or other entries you have overlooked) then press [F9]. A window will appear which will enable you to make entries to take this into account and to post it through to the ledger. The entries required are standard – with the exception of the "Receipt/Payment" box – enter here the Gross value of the transaction, and the program will calculate the VAT in accordance with the Tax Code you have also just entered.

After you have completed this procedure, press [Esc], and you will be asked if you want to: **P**ost **E**dit or **A**bandon this. All postings will be made automatically, and they will be marked as cleared items.

Finally, check if the value in the statement box is the same as that at the end of your bank statement. If it is, proceed as under. If not, then you must find where an error has been made and put it right.

Hit [Esc], and you are then offered the opportunity of clearing the reconciled transactions. The default is 'Y' for Yes, but you may enter 'N' for No if you are not completely happy.

There is also an additional feature to this in Version 5 entitled:

Bank Statement

Select **Nominal Ledger/Bank Statement**. You will presented with a screen which will enable you to select the options you require to print out a copy of all unreconciled transactions on each bank account in use. You may restrict this to certain dates and accounts if you so wish.

Assuming that you have now found it and everything now balances we can proceed to:

VAT Reconciliation

Select **Nominal Ledger/VAT Report** and printout using the defaults offered.

Also select **Nominal Ledger/Control Accounts/Tax Control** and print this out too.

Each of these should enable you to arrive at the same figure for the VAT due.

The VAT printout will give you input and output tax totals. This should agree with the Tax Control figure.

Here again, if there is not agreement, then you MUST locate the reason and correct it before proceeding further.

Reasons for error could be:

An incorrect date being entered.

An incorrect Tax Code being entered on a transaction.

Wrongly using the Tax Code for a Nominal Code posting.

Before going on, once you have rectified the problems, take the following action:

Look (in the Trial Balance) at the value showing for Code 2200 – or whatever you have used for Tax Control.

Take a note of this and then proceed to make a Journal Entry as follows:

If the Tax Control shows a credit balance, make a debit entry to 2200 and an equal credit balance to 2201 (the VAT liability account). If it is a debit balance, then the reverse will apply.

This action has the effect of 'emptying' the 2200 account ready for next month's entries, and accumulating the amount due in 2201. When you eventually pay (or receive a payment from) Customs & Excise then it is made (as a T9 entry) in 2201.

To enable you to complete the VAT return at the end of the quarter, you may care to use the form found in the Appendix of this book. This keeps a control for each month and enables you to easily complete the return.

 Again Version 5 has made considerable changes to this routine, which should make the procedure that much easier.

Select **Nominal Ledger/VAT Return Analysis.**

Then appears the following screen:

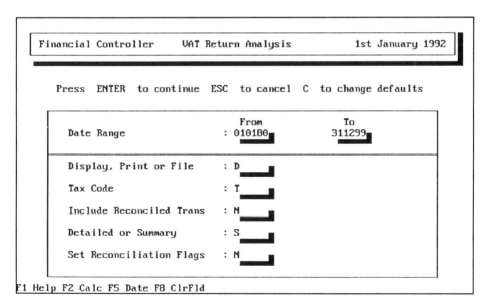

Figure 13.2 VAT Return Analysis Opening Screen

Let us comment on the items one by one:

Date Range: Normally you may accept the defaults since you want to include all transactions irrespective of their date. Other possibilities may be entered here if desired.

Display, Printer or File: The options are as previously discussed.

Tax Code: Again, normally you would accept the default of 'T' to include all codes from T0 to T9. Only if you have a special code outside of this would you normally enter something else here.

Tax by Invoice of Payment: This only appears if you have opted for the Cash Accounting scheme, in which case the default of 'P' for payment is offered.

Include Reconciled Trans: You would normally accept the offered option of 'N' since you would not really have any reason to include items previously reconciled.

Detailed or Summary: The Summary ('S') show the analysis of VAT by code, totalled according to the box on the standard VAT return.

A Detailed Return would include details of each transaction actually included in the return, in case some should not be so included.

Set Reconciliation Flags: Saying 'yes' to this will have the system set a flag against all the items included on this report so that they can be excluded from future reports.

In the event that the system finds some entries before the period you are currently reconciling which have not been included, it will advise you of this fact and ask whether they should be included in this report or not. Normally you should say 'yes' to this, of course.

When you have done all of this, then you will get either a printed VAT report or the same on screen. This is similar in layout to the standard Customs & Excise VAT return, so you should be able to transfer the figures directly to it after having made some checks for accuracy first!

```
┌──────────────────────────────────────────────────────────────┐
│  ┌──────────────────────────────────────────────────────────┐ │
│  │ Financial Controller    VAT Return Analysis    4th March 1992 │
│  └──────────────────────────────────────────────────────────┘ │
│                                                                │
│  For the period 010180 to 311299                     £    P    │
│ ┌────────────────────────────────────────────────────────────┐│
│ │VAT due in this period on Sales           1      11581 ¦ 76  ││
│ ├────────────────────────────────────────────────────────────┤│
│ │VAT reclaimed in this period on Purchases  2       138 ¦ 20  ││
│ ├────────────────────────────────────────────────────────────┤│
│ │Net VAT to be paid or reclaimed by you     3     11443 ¦ 56  ││
│ └────────────────────────────────────────────────────────────┘│
│ ┌────────────────────────────────────────────────────────────┐│
│ │Total value of sales, excluding VAT        4     48827 ¦ 00  ││
│ ├────────────────────────────────────────────────────────────┤│
│ │Total value of purchases, excluding VAT    5      6233 ¦ 00  ││
│ └────────────────────────────────────────────────────────────┘│
│ ┌────────────────────────────────────────────────────────────┐│
│ │Total value of all sales to EC member states  6      0 ¦ 00  ││
│ ├────────────────────────────────────────────────────────────┤│
│ │Total value of purchases from EC member states 7     0 ¦ 00  ││
│ └────────────────────────────────────────────────────────────┘│
│                                                                │
│F1 Help F2 Calc                                                 │
└──────────────────────────────────────────────────────────────┘
```

Figure 13.3 VAT Return Form

The 'Net VAT to be reclaimed or paid by you' figure on this return MUST equal the figure the balance on the Tax Control account (provided you are not using the Cash Accounting scheme). If it does not, you must not proceed further until the reason is established. The above comments about prior versions will help in sorting this out.

Print Out Reports

Before you take this next step, check that your printer is loaded with sufficient paper and that it is switched on.

Now we are going to proceed to take all the reports that we need for record keeping purposes. These may be done in any order you like, and the most logical is to take each of the ledgers in turn and print out from there. However, in practice this means that you have to search a little for the relevant information you need. Therefore you may prefer to follow the order which is suggested below.

Once the printouts have been completed it would make sense to file them in an orderly fashion. Binders can be obtained which will take 'unburst' (i.e. not separated horizontally at the perforations) stationery, and it would be logical to give each type of printout a separate division of the binder e.g. all Sales Day Books together, all Bank Account printouts together etc.

However, choose a method which suits your company best and then stick to it.

The order of printout we suggest is as follows:

1. Sales Ledger

a) Account Balances (Aged) – take 2 copies, one for the record and one for chasing up overdue accounts

b) Transaction History – in essence, your 'Ledger Card' for each account (is a matter of personal choice whether you have each account starting a new page or not; the option is available)

c) Daybooks – essential printouts

2. Purchase Ledger

a) Account Balances Aged – take two copies, one for the record and one for making decisions as to who shall be paid

b) Transaction History

c) Daybooks

3. Nominal Ledger

a) Trial Balance

b) Transaction History – a total printout of all transactions on each account of the Nominal Ledger – it is unlikely that you will want to start a new page for each account here, but you have the option.

c) Control Account History:

   i)   Debtors Control

   ii) Creditors Control

   iii) Bank Account

   iv) Cash Account

   v)   Tax Account

d) Daybooks

e) VAT Return – this is the final one for the record after you have completed the reconciliation and Journals previously mentioned.

We are now also going to mention the Stock Control printouts that are required even though we have not dealt with these aspects in the preceding text.

4. Stock Control (all under 'Stock Reports' sub-menu)

a) Stock Details report – not necessarily produced every month, since it lists all the details of everything in the Stock Control

b) Stock History Report – shows items where movements have taken place

c) Stock Valuation Report – gives the valuation of stock based on quantity of each item times average unit cost.

d) Stock Profit – This Month – a very valuable report giving many good statistical values

e) Stock Profit – Year to Date

f) Stock Explosion – a break down of individual components in made-up stock

g) Re-Order Level Report – a most comprehensive report signalling items that need to be re-ordered, and the supplier reference etc.

Back Up Procedures for different versions of SAGE

At this point, you need to know what version of SAGE you have. The original disk labels should give you this. If you have Version 4.2 onward: you may proceed as below.

If you have an earlier version, then you must first EXIT from SAGE. Nov take a blank, formatted diskette and place it in Drive A. At the C> Promp type:

`COPY \SAGE\COMPANY0\ACCDATA\*.DTA A:\ (or *.DAT if you have a much earlier version)`

and wait until the copying is finished. Then:

Label this disk "xxxxx Month End Disk" where "xxxxx" is the name of th month you have just completed.

Now, for security reasons, take another copy of this same disk and keep in a second secure place.

You can now load up SAGE again and proceed as follows.

Profit & Loss and Budget Reports

Proceed to **Nominal Ledger/Monthly Accounts/P&L and Balanc Sheet.**

You will then see the message:

`Press [ESC] to finish, [CR] to continue.`

Next the following instruction will be seen:

`Insert last month's disk into drive [A] and press [CR].`

If this is the first month you are running this routine then insert any blai formatted disk. Thereafter take the previously month's disk (the creating which we have described above) and insert it into Drive A.

You will now have printed out a complete Profit & Loss and Balance Shee showing This Month and Year to Date figures.

Thence, if you have also set up the Budget figures, proceed to 'Budget Report' which has identical operating procedures to the Profit and Loss report.

Versions from 4.2 onwards

From Version 4.2 onwards, the need to make a monthly data disk has been obviated. The system now enables you to save the required files to the hard disk and recall them from there at month end.

So as part of the Month End routines, select Create Month End File and SAGE will automatically produce the necessary copies.

Thereafter, when running Month End Profit & Loss and Budget Reports, the step to insert a floppy disk will no longer be requested.

 In this version of SAGE, the 'Create Month End' files has been transferred to the Utilities section, and included under the 'Month End' sub-menu.

Produce Statements and Remittance Advices

Next, we need to produce Statements for overdue accounts, and Remittance Advice sheets (optional) for suppliers we are going to pay. We have left these to last since they require a change of stationery, and this is best done now.

We have explained the procedures in both the Sales and Purchase Ledger sections, so proceed as instructed to obtain these documents.

Reconfiguration

Finally the Reconfiguration routine should be actioned, as described earlier. (But see the comments about Version 5 under Trial Balance (q.v.))

Then, and only then, is SAGE ready to receive your next month's input.

The above procedures can now be summarised in the following check list:

❏ Make initial back-up.

❏ Complete all posting for month.

❑ Run Disk Doctor and correct as needed.

❑ Take Bank Account print-out and reconcile and adjust as necessary.

❑ Take VAT printout and reconcile and adjust as necessary.

❑ Take Sales Ledger printouts (except Statements).

❑ Take Purchase Ledger printouts (except remittance Advices).

❑ Take Nominal Ledger printouts (except Month End reports).

❑ Take Stock Control printouts.

❑ Make Month End data disk (internally or externally according to version).

❑ Take Profit & Loss, and Budget printouts.

❑ Produce Statements and Remittance Advices as required.

❑ Reconfigure.

| **V 5** | We mentioned earlier that Version 5 provides for two types of Trial Balance: Current and Reconfigured. |

If you are using the former, then the above scheme is to be followed.

If you are using Reconfigured, then you should run the reconfiguration routine BEFORE taking the Profit & Loss printout. Produce the Month End files after the above print out.

Year End Procedures

Whilst vitally important, they are comparatively simple and mostly automated by SAGE.

The steps are as follows:

1. Complete Month End procedures as above, including Reconfiguration

2. Take two Back-ups and label 'Year End.'

3. Select 'Year End' from Utilities menu and proceed as directed

4. If you are using the Stock Control features, also now select 'Stock Year End'

5. Set Sales & Purchase Ledger Turnover figures to Zero using 'Global Changes' as previously described.

6. Adjust Budget figures as you wish, again using 'Global Changes'.

7. Run another Reconfiguration

You are now ready to begin a new year of entries.

 With Version 5 the procedure is slightly different:

Firstly, when you are ready to run the routine you should first exit Sage and then reload the program, entering the year end date as the system date.

Then run the routine.

14

Use of 'Periscope' in Financial Controller

If you have SAGE Financial Controller, then you have a very useful facility in the form of the 'Periscope' utility.

This enables you to access the information in SAGE even when you are in another program!.

Can you imagine, for instance, being in a word processing program, and a customer rings up with a query on his account? Normally, you would have to save the file you are in, exit the program, load up SAGE, choose Sales Ledger and then Transaction History for this account! Quite a job.

Instead, if you could load up this enquiry function just by pressing a few keys and get immediate access to the account you wanted, think how much time you would save. Then when you finish, you can carry straight on with your Word Processing.

Well this is what Periscope does for you.

Let's see how it works.

Preparation

It is necessary while in the SAGE directory (and before loading SAGE) to type the command "VIEW", and then, when asked, the password that allows you access to these functions.

However, instead of remembering to do this every time, you could include 'VIEW' as a line in your AUTOEXEC.BAT file so that it is loaded when you 'boot' up the computer every morning.

To load

Quite simply, you need to press the following three keys together:
'ALT' 'A' '[CR]'

The key combination in Version 5 is 'ALT' '[CR]'

This will result in the following window appearing over the program you are currently working on:

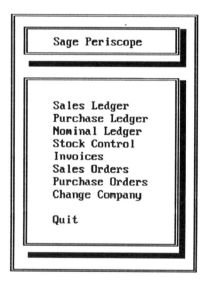

Figure 14.1: Periscope Main Menu

Using Periscope

You may select any of the ledgers by either moving the cursor to the one you wish or by typing the initial letter thereof, and then pressing [CR].

We now detail what information can be obtained when you select the various headings.

Sales or Purchase Ledger

You are firstly presented with a screen similar to the New Account Screen in the Sales Ledger.

Enter in the 'Account Reference' box the code you use. (If you cannot remember exactly the Code, type in the first few letters and SAGE will try to find it for you). If you do not know it at all, use 'PgDn' key to browse through the whole ledger until you find the one you want.

Then this information is presented to you:

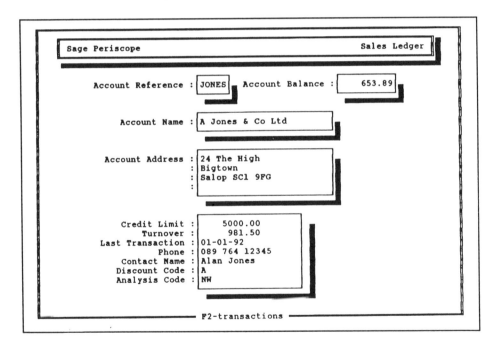

Sage Periscope   Sales Ledger

Account Reference : JONES   Account Balance :   653.89

Account Name : A Jones & Co Ltd

Account Address : 24 The High
                : Bigtown
                : Salop SC1 9FG
                :

Credit Limit :   5000.00
Turnover :   981.50
Last Transaction : 01-01-92
Phone : 089 764 12345
Contact Name : Alan Jones
Discount Code : A
Analysis Code : NW

F2-transactions

Figure 14.2: Sales Ledger Screen 1

By pressing key [F2] additional current information can be displayed as shown in Figure 14.3:

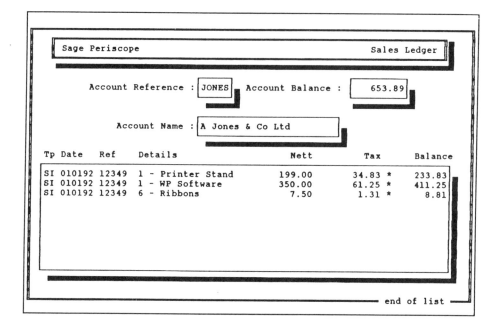

Figure 14.3: Sales Ledger Screen 2

As you can see all the information you could possibly need to answer a telephone enquiry is there for your perusal (the star alongside entries indicates it is unpaid; a small 'p' indicated that it has been paid in this period).

The Nominal Ledger

This may not be used as much, but can still save some time.

Pressing [F2] will obtain detailed breakdowns of the transactions on the relevant accounts.

Other features

It is also possible to access information from the Stock Control, Invoicing, and Sales & Purchase Order processing modules, if used, all using the same principle.

Figure 14.4: Nominal Ledger Screen 1

Additionally, if you have accounts for several companies on SAGE you may select the appropriate one by the 'Change Company' menu which produces this screen:

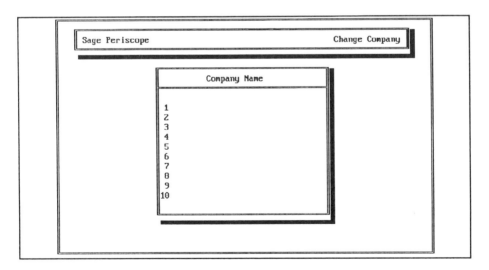

Figure 14.5: Change Company menu

Quitting Periscope

Simply choose "Quit" from the main menu to be returned to the program you are currently working on.

Important Note

It is important to recognize that Periscope is purely an enquiry feature to establish current information.

There is no way that ENTRIES can be made into SAGE when using this feature.

However, we believe that you will use this feature often in the average office and that it is worth while familiarising yourself with the routines involved.

15

Summary

We have now covered the major parts of the functioning of SAGE Financial Controller.

By now you should have a good working knowledge of the system and how to use it for your company. With experience you should be able to see other ways in which to utilise its many features.

It only remains to discuss how to use the information you have retrieved from SAGE. And this in itself is an 'art', and we would strongly recommend that before you make any financial or other decisions based on the figures you have obtained, you obtain professional advice on the interpretation of these figures.

However, there are certain areas where you can make day-to-day decisions using SAGE's reports.

The most obvious is in the matter of Overdue Accounts.

Because of the Aged Debtors report you can obtain whenever you want there is no excuse not to keep abreast of this task. Cash-flow is the 'lifeblood' of any company and it is essential that debts are not left outstanding too long. In fact it can cost you money to have overdue accounts – either in loss of Working Capital for essential purchases, or in Bank interest to keep solvent.

The next area is in the matter of expenditure. Before deciding whether money can be spent on some new project or equipment it is vital to establish what the assets and liabilities of the company are.

The assets can be divided up into:

> Fixed Assets – such as vehicles and equipment. Be realistic in establishing a market value for them, not just the 'written down' value in the accounts.
>
> Debtors – money owed to you by customers
>
> Bank & Cash – assets readily available
>
> Stock – value of such

The liabilities can be divided up into:

> Creditors – suppliers to whom you owe money
>
> Tax Control & VAT Liability – how much money you owe on VAT
>
> PAYE – how much deducted tax you owe
>
> National Insurance – liabilities here
>
> Bank loans – money still to be paid
>
> H P Debts – total liabilities here
>
> Corporation or Schedule D Tax – an estimate based on profits to date of how much you would expect to pay.

Having established these facts, you may then have an indication of whether extra expenditure can be incurred without running the company into financial problems

The use of the Budget report can also be very helpful. Assuming that the figures have been realistically established, every month you will have a printout of your performance against the Budget, with the percentage variation shown. This will be both for the month current and the year-to-date. This therefore means that you can take remedial action at a very early stage if performance should fall below that expected. This is an extremely useful management tool which should be fully utilised.

Various other information and reports (some within the Report Generator which we have not dealt with in this publication) can be used which, amongst other things, will tell you which are your top customers, your turnover with each supplier (perhaps to enable you to negotiate better terms!), which stock items are used the most and which the least... and much else.

SAGE is a valuable and vital management tool. Use it well and it will serve you well and help you to get control of your business. So perhaps when the Managing Director says "Let's computerise the accounts", it will be welcomed!.

Appendix

The following pages list:

Bank reconciliation form
VAT calculation sheet

```
                        BANK RECONCILIATION

FOR No. ................. Account        Month of .................


Closing balance BANK STATEMENT  No: .........           ┌──────────────┐
                                                        │          :   │
                                                        └──────────────┘

LESS cheques raised but not on Statement as follows:

No: .................... for .........:.....
No: .................... for .........:.....
No: .................... for .........:.....
No: .................... for .........:.....
No: .................... for .........:.....
No: .................... for .........:.....
No: .................... for .........:.....
No: .................... for .........:.....
No: .................... for .........:.....
No: .................... for .........:.....
No: .................... for .........:.....
No: .................... for .........:.....
No: .................... for .........:.....
No: .................... for .........:.....
No: .................... for .........:.....
No: .................... for .........:.....
No: .................... for .........:.....
No: .................... for .........:.....
No: .................... for .........:.....
No: .................... for .........:.....

              TOTAL  ┌───────────┐        Adjusted Total  ┌───────────┐
                     │       :   │                        │       :   │
                     └───────────┘                        └───────────┘


PLUS money deposited but not on Statement:

       On .................... for .........:....
       On .................... for .........:....
       On .................... for .........:....
       On .................... for .........:....
       On .................... for .........:....
       On .................... for .........:....
       On .................... for .........:....
       On .................... for .........:....
       On .................... for .........:....
       On .................... for .........:....
       On .................... for .........:....
       On .................... for .........:....
       On .................... for .........:....
       On .................... for .........:....
       On .................... for .........:....

                       TOTAL  ┌───────────┐┌───────────┐
                              │       :   ││       :   │
                              └───────────┘└───────────┘


ADJUSTED STATEMENT BALANCE:  ┌───────────────┐
                             │          :    │  ┐(These totals should be
                             └───────────────┘  │ the same IF no errors
COMPUTER PRINT OUT BALANCE:  ┌───────────────┐  │ have been made)
                             │          :    │  ┘
                             └───────────────┘
```

Figure A.1: Bank Reconciliation Form.

V A T CALCULATION SHEET FOR COMPUTERISED ACCOUNTING SYSTEMS
Period .... to ....

	MONTH	MONTH	MONTH	QUARTER'S TOTAL
OUTPUT TAX				
From printout	:	:	:	:
LESS disallowed amounts	:	:	:	:
Adjusted total	:	:	:	:
PLUS Scale Charge	▨	▨	▨	
[A]	:	:	:	:

INPUT TAX				
From printout	:	:	:	:
LESS disallowed amounts	:	:	:	:
Adjusted total [B]	:	:	:	:

AMOUNT OF VAT DUE

[A] - [B]	:	:	:	:

OUTPUTS

From printout				
LESS disallowed amounts				
Adjusted total [C]				

INPUTS

From printout				
LESS disallowed amounts				
Adjusted total [D]				

Quick checks for accuracy
----

1. Do totals of TAX CONTROL print outs for the three months in question equal the total tax figures above (not allowing for Scale Charge)?
2. Do totals in Tax Control and Tax Liability accounts equal this figure?

Figure A.2: VAT Record Form.

INDEX

Words for the wise - from
Sigma Press

Sigma publish what is probably the widest range of computer books from any independent UK publisher. And that's not just for the PC, but for many other popular micros – Atari, Amiga and Archimedes – and for software packages that are widely-used in the UK and Europe, including Timeworks, Deskpress, Sage, Money Manager and many more. We also publish a whole range of professional-level books for topics as far apart as IBM mainframes, UNIX, computer translation, manufacturing technology and networking.

A complete catalogue is available, but here are some of the highlights:

Amstrad PCW
The Complete Guide to LocoScript and Amstrad PCW Computers – Hughes – £12.95
LocoScripting People – Clayton and Clayton – £12.95
The PCW LOGO Manual – Robert Grant – £12.95
Picture Processing on the Amstrad PCW – Gilmore – £12.95
See also Programming section for *Mini Office*

Archimedes
A Beginner's Guide to WIMP Programming – Fox – £12.95
See also: *Desktop Publishing on the Archimedes* and *Archimedes Game Maker's Manual*

Artificial Intelligence
Build Your Own Expert System – Naylor – £11.95
Computational Linguistics – McEnery – £14.95
Introducing Neural Networks – Carling – £14.95

Beginners' Guides
Computing under Protest! – Croucher – £12.95
Alone with a PC – Bradley – £12.95
The New User's Mac Book – Wilson – £12.95
PC Computing for Absolute Beginners – Edwards – £12.95

DTP and Graphics
Designworks Companion – Whale – £14.95
Ventura to Quark XPress for the PC – Wilmore – £19.95
Timeworks Publisher Companion – Morrissey – £12.95
Timeworks for Windows Companion – Sinclair – £14.95
PagePlus Publisher Companion – Sinclair – £12.95
Express Publisher DTP Companion – Sinclair – £14.95
Amiga Real-Time 3D Graphics – Tyler – £14.95
Atari Real-Time 3D Graphics – Tyler – £12.95

European and US Software Packages
Mastering Money Manager PC – Sinclair – £12.95
Using Sage Sterling in Business – Woodford – £12.95
Mastering Masterfile PC – Sinclair – £12.95
All-in-One Business Computing (Mini Office Professional) – Hughes – £12.95

Game Making and Playing
PC Games Bible – Matthews and Rigby – £12.95
Archimedes Game Maker's Manual – Blunt – £14.95
Atari Game Maker's Manual – Hill – £14.95
Amiga Game Maker's Manual – Hill – £16.95
Adventure Gamer's Manual – Redrup – £12.95

General

Music and New Technology – Georghiades and Jacobs – £12.95
Getting the Best from your Amstrad Notepad – Wilson – £12.95
Computers and Chaos (Atari and Amiga editions) – Bessant – £12.95
Computers in Genealogy – Isaac – £12.95
Multimedia, CD-ROM and Compact Disc – Botto – £14.95
Advanced Manufacturing Technology – Zairi – £14.95

Networks

$25 Network User Guide – Sinclair – £12.95
Integrated Digital Networks – Lawton – £24.95
Novell Netware Companion – Croucher – £16.95

PC Operating Systems and Architecture

Working with Windows 3.1 – Sinclair – £16.95
Servicing and Supporting IBM PCs and Compatibles – Moss – £16.95
The DR DOS Book – Croucher – £16.95
MS-DOS Revealed – Last – £12.95
PC Architecture and Assembly Language – Kauler – £16.95
Programmer's Technical Reference – Williams – £19.95
MS-DOS File and Program Control – Sinclair – £12.95
Mastering DesqView – Sinclair – £12.95

Programming

C Applications Library – Pugh – £16.95
Starting MS-DOS Assembler – Sinclair – £12.95
Understanding Occam and the transputer – Ellison – £12.95
Programming in ANSI Standard C – Horsington – £14.95
Programming in Microsoft Visual Basic – Penfold – £16.95
For LOGO, *see Amstrad PCW*

UNIX and mainframes

UNIX – The Book – Banahan and Rutter – £11.95
UNIX – The Complete Guide – Manger – £19.95
RPG on the IBM AS/400 – Tomlinson – £24.95

HOW TO ORDER

Prices correct for 1993.
Order these books from your usual bookshop, or direct from:

SIGMA PRESS,
1 SOUTH OAK LANE,
WILMSLOW, CHESHIRE, SK9 6AR

PHONE: 0625 – 531035; FAX: 0625 – 536800

PLEASE ADD £1 TOWARDS POST AND PACKING FOR ONE BOOK.
POSTAGE IS FREE FOR TWO OR MORE BOOKS.

CHEQUES SHOULD BE MADE PAYABLE TO **SIGMA PRESS.**

ACCESS AND VISA WELCOME – 24 HOUR ANSWERPHONE SERVICE.